Note:

This is mostly pretend.

That's Life![1]

by Cecil Bothwell

Brave Ulysses Books
2023

---

1 A sexually transmitted, invariably fatal distemperature.

That's Life   ISBN: 9978-1-0881-1246-5
Copyright © 2023 by Cecil Bothwell
All rights reserved/ Cover design by the author/Photo by Dad
Brave Ulysses Books
Asheville, North Carolina 28802

also by the author

- *Gorillas in the Myth: A Duck Soup Reader*
2000/second edition 2008
- *The Icarus Glitch: Another Duck Soup Reader*
2001
- *Finding Your Way in Asheville*
2005/2007/2009/2013/2015
- *The Prince of War: Billy Graham's Crusade for a Wholly Christian Empire*
2007/ 2nd Edition 2009/ 3rd Edition 2021
- *Garden My Heart: Organic Strategies for Backyard Sustainability*
2008
- *Pure Bunkum: Reporting on the life and crimes of Buncombe County Sheriff Bobby Lee Medford*
2008
- *Can we have archaic and idiot? 2, A collection of fictitious tropes*
2009
- *Whale Falls: An exploration of belief and its consequences*
2010
- *She Walks On Water: a novel*
2013
- *Usin' the Juice: Songs, Sermons & Soliloquies*
2017
- *Fifty Wheys to Love Your Liver: Another collection of fictitious tropes*
2018
- *Seize You on the Dark Side of the Moo: Still more fictitious tropes*
2019
- *Waist Not, Want Knot*
2020
- *Self Evident: We hold these tooths*
2021
- *Cede Catalogue: giving it all away*
2021
- *Lucky Breaks (breaking good)*
2022

That's Life!
(as we "know" it)

(Title repeated here in case it slipped your mind
while marveling at the list on the preceding page.)

pour Michele

(il n'y a personne que j'admire plus)

> "Often during the shelling, the guys make jokes and tell funny stories. Humor is very helpful for dealing with stress."
>
> **Ukranian rifleman and medic Ygor Firsov**
> New York Times
> 7 March, 2023

> "Humor is the match I strike to see where I must go, especially when my vision is blurred by sorrow."
>
> **Terry Tempest Williams**
> *Erosion: Essays of Undoing*
> 2019, 2020

[2]

> "Life is like a sewer: what you get out of it depends entirely on what you put into it."
>
> **Tom Lehrer**
> *An Evening Wasted With Tom Lehrer*
> 1959

---

2 Isn't it fascinating to discover a footnote *sans référence?*

Foreword

This is the 5th book of short stories I have completed since COVID-19 landed in our laps.[3] Regarding which, being alone with a laptop seemed like a fairly safe place to ride out much of the storm. As for the title, well nothing like a marvelously infectious, commonly fatal disease to get one thinking about mortality.

These 5 comprise a continuation of two earlier clumps, altogether forming a sort of "body of work" which many agree could use more exercise. [To wit: Lots of people opening and closing, opening and closing.] To that end the book in your hand right now contains 20 General Rules for Living! Yes, 20!

And duly noted: this one has taken longer than the others, perhaps because it is More Important. Twelve months start to finish, plus or minus a day.

We're living in strange days indeed ["Most peculiar Momma" as John Lennon® sang it]—stranger than anything in my 72 years, at least.[4] Obviously enough this is my first pandemic, which alone would weird out any normal person—and my impression (I think a common one and as likely to be wrong as right) is that I'm fairly normal. You'll form an opinion of your own soon enough..

The Republican party in this country seems to have completely left the tracks. I mean Q-Anon? Jewish space lasers?

Their only discernible policies involve lies, accusations and blocking anything that smacks of progress.

The other side of that coin is to give Democrats cover. Oh, gosh, they'd really like to raise wages, tax corporations, ensure voting rights, provide universal health insurance, and cut military spending ... but those damned Republicans!

The monster in the closet is this climate thing which we may find some way to tame if we could agree that the future is worth having. It isn't pretty. Just this morning (6 March, 2023) the *New York Times*® reported that the population of sunflower sea stars out west (AKA: starfish-see back cover) has been wiped out by disease over the past few years, an epidemic thought to be linked to rising ocean temperatures.

"So what?" I hear some among you thinking.

Here's what. Those 24-limbed babies are the chief predator of sea urchins.

---

3   There's a list a few pages back if you missed it.
4   Per Wikipedia®, Cecil Bothwell (born 16 October 1950) is an <u>American</u> politician, writer, artist, musician and builder.

"So what?" I hear again. [You'll see as you slide downslope on this mountain of verbiage that I count on readers to keep the convo going.]

Here's what. The population of sea urchins off the Pacific coast has multiplied 10,000 times in just the past few years.

"So what?"

Sea urchins are wiping out the kelp forests that undergird much of the life in the ocean. Kelp gone, animals gone, ocean dies, and the rest of us with it. Optimistic scientists are trying to develop sunflower sea stars that are resistant to whatever is killing them. Meanwhile scuba divers are using hammers to bust up urchins.

What wouldn't Charles Dickens do with that?

Of course we all know that oceans have a huge effect on the weather—*el niño* and *la niña* for just one famous pair. And the warming seas don't just affect sea stars. They contribute to monsoons and droughts, typhoons and hurricanes.

Then too, when the Greenland icecap melts—which it probably will if we don't find fixes fast—sea level will rise about 25 feet, drowning a majority of the major cities on the globe, at which point the denizens thereof will presumably flee to the interiors, where drought will have eradicated the food supply. Good luck with that.

But maybe we're smarter than we seem.

Until our looming demise dismisses us, perhaps a little humor and some General Rules (20! In case you skipped the second graf upslope.) will make this circus a bit more tolerable.

Cecil Bothwell
Asheville

Mid-March, 2023

Enduring Contents
(To the extent that anything actually endures.)

High Assembly Objects	13
Mattress People?	20
Broken Cross	28
Going Viral	30
Petri Dish	31
Warm Mud	35
Before You Die	38
Half-life	42
Down Among The Ruins	44
Time After Time	47
Teach a ~~man~~ person to fish	50
It's the little things	53
Born and razed	57
World enough. And time	60
Thanks. For the memories.	62
Events leading up to ...	67
Growth	71
If at first ...	73
Irked	75
Swim-Swam-Swum	79
Oh, wow!	84
Mystery Solved	88
Suite Dreams	90
Short Sharp Shock	94
Upper crust	97
Möbius B	103
Title	106
Perceptibly paler	110
"In the town where I was born"	113
Into each life ...	120
The week that wasn't	125
Distance is gone	128
Will we find out	133
Too little, two late	138
Extirpated[2]	142

More earthworms!	146
Alone on a hill	150
Rustication	153
How high is up?	156
Purr	159
Robovac	161
Extremities	165
But what?	166
Geocaching®	169
Early squirrels and late	172
Octopied	175
Geocaching®^{2}	177
The problem with earthworms	180
The long and the short of it	184
Book Club Questions	197
Author interview	198
Shameless commerce page	199
Page left blank in order to inform readers the end is near	200

High Assembly Objects

You're probably thinking "smart phone" or "rocket" or "sky scraper" right about now, but I don't want us to get started on the wrong foot. You head down that rabbit hole and the signal strength between writer and reader will precipitously diminish.

What we're dealing with here is ourselves—ever and always the most pertinent subjects in our peripatetic lives.[5] Also, "them."

If and when—very likely when, though exactly when is problematic—we do meet "them," they too will be "high assembly objects." Right? Otherwise, how in hell did they get here? Even if they do a Star Trek® "beam me down Scotty," they'll have to reassemble, (though one supposes that beaming down results in a "low reassembly" of a high assembly object.)

The problem, as Terry ponders it, is whether or not we'd even recognize alien assemblages as high-end in the first place. Sure, if they're quadrupedal in some fashion, and grey-green, and sport inverted pear-shaped noggins ... no question. But, here's the thing. Having four limbs *seems* pretty handy to we who have achieved some measure of dexterity, availing ourselves of same, yet it is the height of parochiality to assume that this is the only way to be.

Consider the neck of a giraffe. See?

What if these highly anticipated extraterrestrials turn out to be shaped like mattresses? Heck, I could be lying on one now and be none the wiser. For that matter, maybe they <u>are</u> already here, undergirding all of us "lucky" enough to have one or a few in our abodes. If an alien race wanted to silently invade there are few ways Terry can imagine that would be subtler than to let the local Mattress Man® outlet distribute your minions.

Then they could study us, up close and personal, learn our deepest secrets, evaluate our strengths and weaknesses, only to rise up at a given signal and take over. This has come to worry Terry to the extent that he mostly sleeps on the floor.

"Go ahead. Laugh." That's what he'd like to tell you, though he wouldn't, as we shall see. "But don't blame me when they rise up and unceremoniously toss everyone hither and yon! A hard, hard reign gonna fall, for certain!" [His Dylan® ref, not mine.]

---

5 To which the "That's" in the book title refers.

(In my experience people who use the phrase "hither and yon" are neither here nor there most of the time. *Moi?*)

It's always troubling to your author when the first protagonist to pop up in a short story collection turns out to be a little bit off-kilter. I mean, yes, my tales always go downhill, but, as the old rule about bobsledding has it: Start At The Top!

Terry must have some redeeming characteristic, though, truth be told, if he's right about the mattresses, we'll all be glad that at least one among us was already down there on the floor, prepping for the irresistible cataclysm.[6]

Terry Jepson's work for the Forest Service® gives him lots of time to ponder Big Questions, and the floor he sleeps on many nights is part of another class of "high assembly objects"—at the top of a very long and winding set of stairs. Yes, a firetower!

(Obviously, high-tech satellite[7] imagery might already have supplanted the need for people in towers, but for the purposes of this little *assemblage*[8] we need him to be there. Okay?)

("Why?" you ask. Stay tuned!)

So, while he spends his days during fire-season[9] scanning the horizon for puffs of smoke, he thinks—about the mattress people currently likely headed our way from *Alpha Centauri,* yes (or the planet Serta®?)— but much, much more. Like you—when giraffe necks were mentioned on the previous page—he marvels at the route taken by their laryngeal nerves. That makes no practical sense, does it? Or, spiders. He wonders if they get bored, just hanging around, stock still, waiting for lunch to arrive. Or Carol. A puzzle within a conundrum if there ever was one.

Carol Saarinen works in the local USFS® office near the trailhead to the tower, implementing the regional management plan, which, predictably enough, is how Terry happens to know her. She's a pro. She's also pleasant, and we all agree that being pleasant is ... well, not to put too fine a point on it ... is *pleasant!*[10]

But she, too, has her quirks, and aren't quirks what make us interesting to each other? Absent quirks we'd all be about as dull as rubber erasers or mattresses. [You can quote me on that.] One

---

6 We'll need a clear-eyed leader at that moment. And as we discover in the next paragraph, "clear-eyed" is a professional asset for our guy.
7 These "high assembly objects" are piling up now!
8 First appearance of *français* in the current volume! We're off to the races!
9 Which we here note is quickly becoming a January to December affair.
10 This isn't *français,* it is italicized for emphasis. [For readers unfamiliar with my writerly *ouvrir,* most italicized words in my work are foreign.]

of her quirks figures significantly in the reason we need Terry to be in a fire tower, but let's not get ahead of ourselves.

Another quirk of hers, by the way, is her inclination to write in boustrophedon. (!)

Carol has a *Schnauzer*[11] named *Schnallen.*[12] The dog goes everywhere with her. Even now—if you're reading this between eight a.m. and four p.m. on a weekday—he's *Schlummern*[13] at her feet while she works on next month's schedule. After-hours and on weekends he's either trotting along beside her as she hikes, sitting beside her in her USFS® pick-up truck, or *Schlummern* at her feet atop either a mattress or an alien (I mean, how would we know the difference?) fear of which neither Carol nor *Schnallen* entertain.

We can infer that her job takes her in a very different direction than Terry's. While he's gazing into the distance pondering Big Questions, she's gazing at a computer screen considering Big Plans. His questions are unbounded by time or space, while her questions have already been answered after long months of study and public input. While her calendar is structured to move in a predictable and orderly fashion from A to B to C, his days are monotony writ large between alarming incidents of potential disaster (!) when careless campers, or thoughtless smokers or evil arsonists trigger a conflagration.

But opposites are said to attract and attraction there has been. Last week, on his way back to the tower, Terry popped in at the office to ask Carol if she'd like to join him for dinner this Saturday. Her reply, typical for one as calendrically disciplined as our character, was, "Sounds good, but I'll need to confirm tomorrow." This was fine with one as uncalendrically attached as Terry and he proceeded to his parked car where he donned his heavily laden backpack, put Tweed[14] on his shoulder, and hiked two miles or so to his place of employ. Whistling.

What he was pondering on that particular day was the single-mindedness of *Champollion,* principle translator of the Rosetta Stone. He had to hand it to him. You know?

But I see a hand up in back.

"Bewstrifi-what?"

Boustrophedon.

---

11 You can tell this is *Deutsch* because it is both capitalized and italicized.
12 "Buckles" in *Deutsch.*
13 Snoozing.
14 His cat.

"Oh."

I think it's not surprising that Terry was fascinated by *Jean-François Champollion*.[15] As a teen *Jean-François* was already fluent in Greek, Latin, Hebrew, Arabic, Amharic, Sanskrit, Syriac, Persian, and Chaldean. Then he tackled Coptic. A bit later, while ill, he asked his brother for a Chinese grammar, to amuse himself during his recovery.

Another hand up?

"Boustrophedon?"

Right.

"No, I mean, what is it?"

It's the way Carol writes in her diary.

"Fine. But what in hell is it?"

Take a chill pill, dude. Interrupting is so, so rude. Sigh.

That means she writes from left to right on the first line and right to left on the second in the manner of an ox pulling a plow across a field, then turning at the end of a row. The term is drawn from the Ancient Greek *bous,* or "ox," and *strophe,* or "turn"— meaning "as the ox turns." This pattern was used for Ancient Greek, Etruscan and a few other languages. It is pretty unusual for English writers, which is why I labeled her "quirky." I dare say, you've not likely run into it before. But now you've learned something new and fascinating, non?

Okay? Okay.[16] It's not easy, but Carol isn't easily daunted.

This reminds me of one of my favorite ideas, something I've written about before, but given my book sales this is going to be new for most of you. Not the boustrophedon thing, I only learned about that this morning.[17] The hieroglyphs and the Rosetta Stone. Hieroglyphs were interpreted by Egyptian priests but while some images represented sounds others represented ideas and you had to know the underlying idea in order for it to make sense.

Like say: ♥ my *Schnauzer*.

That's super simple, of course, compared to a thousand images on the side of an obelisk. But here's what I am driving at. In a phenomenal book, *The Origin of Consciousness in the Breakdown of the Bicameral Mind*,[18] by the Princeton psychologist, psychohistorian and consciousness theorist Julian

---

15 See how much more *français* the name sounds typed in italics?
16 Notice that this bit of boustrophedon includes both Ελληνικά (Greek) and *français*.
17 About 4:30 a.m., 12 March, 2022.
18 Houghton Miflin, Mariner Books, 1976

Jaynes, the author posits that human consciousness emerged with the invention of alphabetic writing.

[Do know that my explanation, based on a book I read forty years ago, is not going to be comprehensive, but I have thought a lot about it over the decades, being inclined, like Terry, to stare into the distance and mull. Mull, mull, mull.]

The era before the emergence of alphabets is often called the Age of Prophecy. That's when people thought they heard gods or seraphim or spirits or burning bushes giving them instructions or advice. (You'd have to think a burning bush would be saying something like, "Water! Water!") In Jaynes' framework that experience was one brain hemisphere communicating with the other: the bicameral "two-chambered" mind—left hemisphere chattering to the right. Because it came to people inside their heads when no one else was speaking to them ... well it had to come from somewhere.

"Izzat you Zeus?"

The thing about an alphabet, with sounds attached to each letter and combination of letters, is that writing became a recording device. I can read the previous sentence out loud (which I do with all my writing because that's the best way to know whether it flows) and you can do the same and make approximately the same sounds (depending on your accent and druthers: i.e. tomayto, tomahto.)

Suddenly people were able to think in terms of written words and discovered that the ideas bouncing around in their noggins were *their own*. From that point on the prophets lost much of their audience. ("Oh, Zeke? He's just talking to himself. A nutter.") Also the high priests lost a lot of status. (Later the mucky-mucks in the Roman Catholic Church® tried to reclaim some glam by insisting the liturgy and so forth was only to be intoned in Latin, regarding which most of their parishioners didn't have a wrinkled clue. "Gosh, it *must* be the Words of God®!" *In Latin!* Oh gosh!)

(And still later "speaking in tongues?" Really?)

It's no surprise that Jaynes was a Unitarian®. But I digress.

Terry was using the self-reflection made possible by his consciousness to ponder his own trajectory. Was he ever going to find *something* that drew him helplessly forward as *Champollion's* pursuit of language had done? When he was honest with himself he had to admit to being more a dreamer than a doer. "Face it," he said aloud as he reached the top step, "It doesn't matter if I'm right about the mattresses from *Alpha*

Centauri, because no one would believe me. Also, if things warm up between me and Carol wood floors are not ideal for diddling."[19]

We see here both self-awareness and a practical bent.

Another hand up in back? It's no wonder this story is dragging. Okay, shoot.

"Giraffe neck? What nerve?"

Laryngeal.

"What about it?"

Were you born in a barn? [Funny how this "put-down" conflicts with, assuming one both deems it a "put-down" and embraces certain religious views, say, the Jesus in a stable thing.]

Anyway for the benighted and confused amongst you: A giraffe's laryngeal nerve goes a long crazy way.[20]

So we see that Terry is hoping that his budding romance with Carol will bloom and grow, such that at some point they will become lovers. Perhaps on a mattress. Or maybe a sofa if he can steer her around the alien landing zones. Maybe a beanbag?

When he read[21] the previous sentence, or more accurately "sentence fragment," Terry became agitated.

True. Beanbag "chairs" are less common than mattresses, but they observe more of our lives, positioned as they are in disparate settings, and also, and more threateningly, when we are settled therein we are totally at their mercy. We might not be tossed aside but rather, absorbed. What if "they" are the "them?"

"Crazy how?"

The beanbags?

"No, the giraffe's whatchamacallit. Why does it go a long crazy way?"

Evolution.

Terry has begun to cast a very wary eye at the beanbags he encounters at friends' homes. And, obviously, if that's the only structural option offered in terms of seating arrangements, he plops down on a rug.

"That is a very unsatisfying answer."

Are you anti-science?

"No. But you can't expect me to accept a one-word answer about something as evidently complex as a giraffe's neck."

---

19 Only on page 18 with footnote 19 coinciding (glad we don't subscribe to numerology in these parts) to discover the first reference to steaminess, for which your author is well known. Stay tuned. Much more to come!
20 Some would say the same about this tale.
21 I always let my characters proofread.

I think it's really obvious, but whatever. The recurrent laryngeal nerve first developed in fish, OK? It went from the brain, looped around the heart, which was, at least in the first fish, probably about an inch or less toward the rear, and then forward to the gills—so maybe a two inch anatomical loop. Max.

Later on some curious fish (lately identified as *Tiktaalik*) climbed up on a beach walking on its fins, like your modern day walking catfish, and discovered that there weren't any predators yet, which was a distinct improvement. So the fins turned into legs and so forth and so on, and the fish turned into dinosaurs who all got wiped out when the big asteroid landed near the Yucatan, but for some little guys the scales had gradually turned into fur and etcetera and etcetera, and eventually they turned out to be kind of like horses but there was a lot of competition for the low hanging fruit and some of them grew long necks. Okay?

So, where was I? The next day, about ten in the morning, Terry heard footfalls on the winding stairs and inferred he had company "coming up." He knew better than to peer down because, due to the spiral, he wouldn't be able to see his visitor until the person reached the last run.

"You didn't really explain the nerve thingy."

Oh, come on. It still loops around the heart so now it's about 15 feet long. Makes no biological sense whatever. It is one of the best examples of unintelligent design.

Anyway, I think it will come as no surprise that Terry's visitor proved to be Carol, though, given that we haven't discussed the status of their relationship it *might* come as a surprise that she hugged and kissed him (!) before saying: ɛɘY

Then she picked up *Schnallen,* who is much better at ascending than its reverse, turned and headed back to her office. And that's why we had to have Terry two miles up a trail and a hundred feet up on a high assembly object. See?

But, hold it. Doesn't that have to be the *second thing* she said? It could be. On the other hand those in love often share little endearments. I suspect Terry is just crazy about the way Carol talks in boustrophedon.[22]

---

22 To tie this all together, the human laryngeal nerve, perhaps two feet long, loops the heart as in our fishy forebears, and is involved in speech as well as protecting your airway when you eat or drink. And Jaynes' theories are still taken very, very seriously by researchers studying ancient history and civilizations and modern psychology. There is method in my madness, whether obvious or not.

Mattress People?

Or beanbag people (to start off on an inclusive note.) Of course I'm using "people" here in the broad sense of intelligent beings, the framework in which we are inclined to define ourselves. One conundrum being: Would we know if we weren't?

The physicists Enrico Fermi, Edward Teller, Herbert York and Emil Konopinski walked into a bar ... but that's a story for a different time. Actually the four of them were walking to lunch in the summer of 1950 just a few months before your author popped into the world. They were discussing the possibility of alien life and faster-than-light travel—the usual chit chat when physicists converge—and agreed that as big as the universe seemed to be, the first was likely and the second at least possible. Then Fermi piped up with something like, "But where is everybody?"

Word got around and Fermi was credited with his very own *paradox*. The thinkers who thought about it decided that if we were *not* alone there must be other technological civilizations out there among the many stars in many galaxies, and probably many much older than ourselves, so their versions of Hitler's radio tirades and "I Love Lucy," and "Survivor" and cigarette ads would be beaming in at us from many light years away. But ... nothing.

So what was the deal?

The two most frequent answers proffered were that either life on earth was completely unique for some imponderable reason, or, that technological civilizations always screwed up and died soon after they invented ball point pens or Velcro® or atomic weapons. Cheerful, eh what? Personally, to be clear, what I think is coolest about Fermi's Paradox is that we share a birth year. It makes me feel connected and, honestly, a little special. Am I not a little "paradoxical," at least viewed in profile?

Professor Lee Cronin, who studies the chemistry of life at the University of Glasgow,[23] speculates that the reason for the Fermi Paradox is not that "they" are not out there, it's just that we can't interact with other life forms because they are so different. (Mattresses? My idea, not his.) Further, that the explanation of the Fermi Paradox is that it starts from the assumption that if there is life out there it would be in substantial ways like life here,

---

23 As of March, 2022, if you're reading this in some far off future.

that our biology is the only biology possible. Or that all roads lead to telecom giants and SuperBowl Sundays® and boxed wine.

This, he observes, is a baseless assumption.

Furthermore, Cronin believes that even if there are earth-like planets, with much the same chemical makeup as our homeplace, and therefrom cooked up similar ribosomes and so forth, evolution is so dependent on chance that it couldn't possibly turn out the same way.

On another front, very strange DNA has been discovered in the Atacama Valley in Chile, unlike any ever seen before. Scientist and author Paul Davies opines that life could have originated on Earth more than once and to this day there could be a "shadow" biosphere that is simply too weird to fit into our definition of Earth life. ["Me and my shadow" ... wrote Al Jolson, Billy Rose and Dave Dreyer. Did they know something we do not?]

As we discussed on page 19, one significant nodal point for our development arrived in the form of a surprise visit from a very large asteroid. Absent that splashdown mammals would probably never have turned into us and there would be *actual* lizard people on TikTok® and Facebook®, not just behave-a-likes.

But if we allow ourselves to be somewhat more imaginative, maybe the basis of life on some other globes is a polyester/cotton blend instead of carbon. (I know polyester and cotton are carbon-based, but this is a "thought experiment." I'm using this example as a hypothetical. I could have posited, say, molybdenum-based life, but then the mattresses would be uncomfortably hard.) So couldn't they have evolved into mattresses? [We could be reclining on aliens at night or sinking into their comfy beany selves and be none the wiser.]

The question then arises, "Okay, smarty-pants, if they're here, they're obviously a few jumps ahead of SpaceX®, so why haven't they said hello?"

There's an answer for that too. I've been talking to Terry about it. He thoughtfully inquired, "When was the last time you tried to explain calculus to an ant?"

He got me there. Maybe the mattresses in our midst are so much more advanced than we are that their attempts at discussion would be as pointless as saying $d/dx^n = nx^{n-1}$ to a member of *Formicidae?*[24] They might not even think of us as

---

[24] First use of Latin in the current volume!

"people."[25] After all, we scurry around doing all kinds of pointless things, wearing ourselves out—not unlike ants—while they just chill. Likely thinking great big thoughts. Maybe communicating telepathically. Musing on the uber ineffable. Playing eight-dimensional chess or nine-dimensional checkers, or, something way more complicated.

This sort of thing pretty much justifies my letting Terry in here—off-kilter or no—in the first place. He gets me going.

But none of that is what this story is about, at least moving forward. This, I think, will have to include Carol, since she's the only other living character involved so far. (Jaynes reached his date of expiry in 1997.) I suppose, given that she's a dog-person, it could involve *Schnallen*. This would give us an opening to introduce another character! Oh, goody! Whence *Schnallen*?

Well, life does what it does, for better or worse. In this case *Schnallen* was a "for better" item before another thing got worse.

Schnallen was a *gift*.

You have to know someone pretty darn well before you even *think* of giving that someone a dog. Pets require responsibility and you are handing that someone ten or fifteen years of it—if all goes well for the pooch—as well as the heartache at the end.

Friedrich is of German ancestry, as you surely could infer, given his name and his breed of choice. As we determined in the previous paragraph he and Carol were—emphasis on the past tense here—close. "Close" to the point that they frequently frolicked in the all-together, though they didn't live together, which proved a great relief to both when they parted. Splitting up is messier for cohabitants.

Interestingly, and perhaps surprisingly, research reported in the February, 2022, issue of *Harper's®,* which I perused yesterday, has revealed that men experience more heartache than women after a breakup. This tells us that Friedrich likely took it harder than Carol, but, honestly, it was *his fault*. If he'd been in bed with just *one* woman when she dropped by that fateful Saturday, that would have been one thing, and there's no way of knowing what her response might have been. Two created a bridge too far, particularly since one of the pair was Carol's sister!

Family Feud® for certain! (Family Freud?)

Riva apologized, but it took a couple of years before Carol came to terms with the whole mess, a resolution made more difficult when Riva moved in with the philanderer. On the flip

---

25 i.e.: intelligent beings.

side, while Carol remained unhappy with the pair, as predicted by the research I read yesterday she was not personally unhappy. She got right over the heart hurt.

Meanwhile she had fallen in love with her *Schnauzer,* in the sense that one might fall in love with a dog, having made the unsurprising discovery that man's best friend can be a woman's BFF as well.[26] [Well, not "forever" forever.]

As noted in our previous story, *Schnallen* is Carol's constant companion. If the pair hadn't clicked and she had handed the pup back to Friedrich, the "best friend" thing would have bumped directly into the male heartache phenom. The dog would have been a constant reminder of both Carol and his own having blown the best relationship he'd ever had. A constant source of lament.

But for Carol? For our protagonist the canine became the silver lining released from the storm cloud that was "what's-his-name." Along the yellow-brick-road of life she and *Schnallen* had now found Terry, who, we recall, like all my best characters is a cat person, but, importantly, is not unkind to dogs.

This brings us to General Rule #1:[27] "In successful new relationships it is best if only one of two candidates has a dog."

"Why?" I hear you asking, even if not aloud.

Dogs are needy.[28] They need the attention of anyone in their near vicinity. It's fine for a conjoined couple to acquire two dogs so the neediness is spread around from the get-go, but if two dog owners get together and the other's dog starts exhibiting that neediness in regard to the new person ... it just doesn't work out. The panting and slobbering and whining almost inevitably drives the participating humans apart, particularly if one of the canines exhibits greater affection for the *other* person. Trust me on this.

So, Carol and Terry are on safe turf, but what about Riva and Friedrich? Despite their moral failing, don't they have some redeeming features? Are they going to "make it?"

So far so good, given that neither arrived in bed on that

---

26 For those of that particular bent. Here at the cat ranch we agree that the dog thing is overworked. There's a cat on my chest as I type these words, purring. Try to teach a dog to purr ... lots of luck!

27 Pretty darn amazing. We're only on page 23 and we've already stated a General Rule, demonstrating that your author is socially responsible. An important function of the current volume—*That's Life* for those of you with memory issues (see the header on this page)—is to offer such.

28 Which is why cats are, IMHO, better companions. They are self-assured and confident and very rarely slobber.

fateful Saturday in possession of a dog. [Corollary #1a:[29] "It is better for neither candidate to have a dog than for both.] On the downside, neither had the inestimable good sense to fraternize with a cat. Being in their late twenties there's still time for that.

As for Celine, the other participant in the fateful frolic, she has two dogs, and after the blow-up decided that three was a crowd so she won't figure in the rest of this story. Maybe later.

Riva is an excellent cook, by the way, which is actually what led to her being in that compromised situation, though of course it hardly justifies it. She had cooked a splendid dinner at Carol's apartment for the three of them and the merry way to a man's heart took it's storied route. When Carol had excused herself to the facilities after the meal, Riva and Friedrich locked eyes as he licked his lips and they both knew the upshot was inevitable. He had a hunger and she had the recipes. It was only a matter of time.

A week, it seems. Rather, less. One Saturday night to the following Saturday morning, implying as it does that it was actually a Friday night sleep-over. General Rule #2: "Philanderers discovered in bed with philanderees[30] in the morning generally landed there the night before."

Taken altogether, what with Carol not being desperately heartbroken and relatively optimistic regarding Terry and/or other potential "replacement parts," Friedrich deeply entrenched in Riva's culinarity, Terry hopeful regarding Carol's affection, *Schnallen Schlummern*[31] at Carol's feet, and Riva not unhappy that Celine had made herself scarce [though you just *know* who invited Celine in the first place, Riva, oh Riva]—we have ourselves a set of happy campers.

Unlike, say, Jimmy Buffet®, who "stepped on a pop-top, cut my heel had to cruise on back home." This, obviously bifurcates.

Cutting one's "heel on a pop-top" is one of those cultural "moments" that obviously didn't endure. During a brief period in the late 20th Century, beverage companies installed throw-away openers in their metal containers. Tug it out and toss it for the next heel to hit on.

Oops. Lawsuits much?

---

29 Oh, we are on a roll! Add Corollary #1b: "The dog rules do not apply regarding cats."
30 Is that a word?
31 Language lessons work best with repetition.

With remarkable speed the packaging industry came up with openers that remained ensconced in the body of the container. [Whew!]

On the other hand, whether or not Buffet actually blew out his flip flop and stepped on a pop-top—one suspects it was a rhyme thing—the ensuing song made him enormously rich.

[Latitude Margaritaville® anyone?[32]]

Leading of late to Latitude Margaritaville® retirement communities. That boy sure knows how to monetize. Set up a space where those "Fins to the left, Fins to the right" Boomers can spend their golden years "wasting away again." I'm not being snide. Jimmy caught the zeitgeist and entertained us all the way down to the goalposts.

In any event, it looks like our little clump of characters are happy just now, so this is probably a good time to wind things up, before one of them steps in it or on it again.

---

32 One of three (and counting) retirement communities Buffet co-owns.

Broken Cross

Way, way, way back, in the Bronze Age, and possibly even before that—because who really knows what went on before people could write important things down?[33]—recall also that this was B.M.[34] so people weren't sleeping well—some clever someone scratched a symbol on a rock. Something like this:

Kind of amazing. Inventing art *and* math at the same time! Sometimes great leaps forward come all at once like that. Of course, numbers were still a long way off, but I think we can all agree that this was a plus. We can just imagine how proud the inscriber would have been, dragging friends over to the limestone cliff-face to see his etching.[35] Sometimes while they were roasting guinea pigs[36] over an open fire, some among the tribe would gaze at the thing and marvel at how it all added up.

Sadly, once the idea of scratching things on dolomite caught on, graffiti became a thing.

I recall hiking in the coastal wilderness in Olympic National Park and finding some scribbles scratched into a rock including the plus sign mentioned above. They were the kind of figures a child might draw. I shook my head and muttered something about people having no respect for an international treasure and spoiling the unspoilt wonder of the place for those of us who came after.

---

33 See page 17. And should it be "write down important things"?
34 Before Mattress.
35 This proto-mathematician may also have invented seduction.
36 Reminding us of "Knot My Problem," on page 26 of the fabulous collection *Waist Not, Want Knot,* Brave Ulysses Books, 2020.

Later, in a visitors' center, I discovered a photograph of the figures accompanied by an explanation of Makah Native American petroglyph art. Oops. [Rush to judgment much?[37]]

So, before long, when Artist #1 was off hunting guinea pigs with his buddies, Artist #2 came by and added a bit to the project. She had just inscribed two lines when she heard the hunters laughing and joking as they came back to camp with their quarry, so she hastened away, not wanting to risk their anger.

卍

"Oh man, somebody wrecked your masterpiece!"
"That is so awful!"
"It's like somebody *subtracted* from it! Two minus signs!"

Artist #1 studied it for a bit, and then looked at the plump guinea pig hanging from the pole supported on the sturdy shoulders of two of the hunters. "I think this brought good luck."

Since Artone had created the image the others had to agree. But the mischief was not over, no no.

The next time the band went off in search of the mighty guinea pig, Artwo snuck back into camp and finished the job.

卐

"Look! They wrecked it again!"
"Bummer, man!"

But Artone looked at it and traced the pattern with a finger, then looked at the three guinea pigs strung on the pole. "I think this brought even better luck."

And so it began. You could reasonably say such ideas added up pretty easily because the symbol or it's reverse was invented and reinvented around the world by tribes and cultures of all sorts —almost always with good meanings attached.

The modern name for the symbol comes from Sanskrit: स्वस्तिक, or *svastika*, meaning "conducive to well-being."

To a tribe in the San Francisco Bay area it represented the four mountains in the four directions, to several southwestern tribes it symbolized good luck, for the Hopi it symbolized the wandering Hopi clan, for the Navajo it was the whirling log of

---

37 Though I'd argue that we can't know if it was art or graffiti in it's time.

healing. Among the plains natives the Dakota regarded it as a solar wheel and said "the year is a circle around the world." For the *Guna* people of *Guna Yala,* Panama, it represents the octopus that created the world (being pre-numeric they couldn't count the arms) and in several Indo-European religions it represents lightning bolts attributable to the thunder god.

In 1920 it was adopted by the U.S. 45th Infantry Division, based in Oklahoma City, as a badge with a yellow swastika on a red diamond, honoring the local Native American population.

Meanwhile it was also in fairly wide use in Europe in the first years of the 20th century, and generally used in a positive framework.

Of course the Nazi's spoiled it for everyone. But how did they happen to adopt the graphic? Historians would have you believe that it had to do with secret societies and the nationalist *völkisch*[38] movement. But, unsurprisingly (one supposes), that's not how I think it landed there.

You see, my father started out as a child. I still have a photo of him astride a pony—when he was small—taken at some sort of dude ranch or tourist camp in South Dakota. He must have been about seven years old. This was before he was hit by a car in East St. Louis t age 8^{39}. My grandfather, from Lagrange, Indiana, and my grandmother from Yankton, were vacationing in her home state, first visiting her parents, then visiting the Yankton Sioux reservation, though, truth be told, I don't suppose they penetrated the reserve much beyond the gift shop.

[This was back in the good old days before America honored the First Peoples by carving the faces of four Great White Fathers on the side of a sacred mountain, so I'm pretty certain my kinfolk didn't traipse over to Rushmore.]

Little Cecil was quite taken by a small sterling spoon fashioned by a Sioux silversmith and my grandparents, in the first flush of Big Cecil's[40] recent promotion decided to spring for it.

Then, too, grandma had just received word that she had passed her audition and would start as pianist with the Chicago Symphony® in the fall. So the flushness was full circle and she decided that a similar spoon would be just the gift for her favorite cousin. In Germany.

That part of the story gets complicated.

---

38 *Deutsch!*
39 He survived! Didn't want to leave you in suspense.
40 Yep. I come from a string of 'em.

Grandma's parents had emigrated to the U.S. from Ukraine, together with most of their village, sometime around 1881, but they were originally German pacifists.

In the 18th century the Holy Roman Empire® was gradually falling apart, but that didn't mean they weren't trying, and trying meant war. At the same time Catherine the Great® over in Russia needed to boost farm production and announced that the children of farmers who settled in Ukraine would never be conscripted into the Russian army. Around that time Napoleon® was headed east toward Prussia, so my anti-war forebears on the German side of the family took Her Greatness up on it. They created a prosperous little village called Нойфельд in Ukranian, but *Neufeld* in *Deutch,* or "new field" in English—which makes perfect sense given their move—and everything was hunky-dory for a century.

But then Tsar Alexander III came to power. He developed a reputation as a peacemaker. His theory was that peacekeeping required a bigger army—and, "Hey! Look at all those strapping *Deutsche* farm boys pitchforking hay in Ukraine!"

Most of my crowd packed up and headed for the Dakota Territory, a landscape and climate not dissimilar to Ukraine. One uncle, however, decided to cleave to cultural roots and go back to Germany, hopeful that the settlement at the end of the Franco-Prussian War would allow a period of quiet.

He and his *frau* had a daughter and both survived World War I, though his wife succumbed to the 1918 influenza epidemic. During those years they had sent the girl to Yankton for safety, and the cousins had grown close.

When the smoke cleared in Europe cousin Paula returned to Munich, which is where she was living when the spoon arrived in the mail. She thought it was a wonderful gift and showed it to her dear friend Franziska Braun and Franziska's eight year old daughter, Eva.

QED.[41]

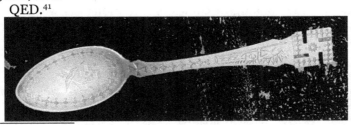

---

41 Of course I made this up (except the spoon) but it gave us the opportunity to discuss so many *interesting* things that I think it was worth it. Don't you?

Going Viral

The initial question, obviously enough, is how a virus fits into a collection called *That's Life,* because it isn't at all clear that viruses are living things. They *can be* insidious, of course, but they don't wiggle or crawl around. Furthermore they don't have cells, they don't reproduce and they don't use energy. Also, they don't seem to respond to their environment outside of binding to receptors on cells and sharing[42] their DNA which causes the host cell to make more viruses—more a catalyst than controller.

Our first paragraph didn't get us any closer to an answer, so it was a waste of pixels, or ink if you are reading a print edition of this little *fabrication.*[43]

It's true that avian flu viruses get coated with calcium while visiting the intestines of birds which makes it more infectious for humans, but it isn't like the virus *intended* to mimic M&Ms® any more than an M&M® has volition. (Not counting the M&M® characters who got a makeover in January of this year, when Mars® announced that the anthropomorphized candy characters will have "more nuanced personalities to underscore the importance of self-expression and power of community through storytelling." Uh huh.)

That paragraph didn't move us along either, and frankly, making the arms and legs of the M&M® characters the *same color* as their candy coating doesn't seem to go a long way toward either nuance, racial equity, truth, justice or the American way.[44]

The thing about "going viral" in the modern sense is that it is very much intentional. People create memes in high hopes that they will "go viral," that others will make copies and pass them along. But that making of copies is intentional as well, whereas when a virus sidles up to a receptor neither the virus nor the cell has any intention whatsoever. So. Where does that leave us?

---

42 "Sharing" sounds active, but it actually just "happens." meaning that it is pretty passive, like, say, second-hand smoke.
43 Italicized so you know we are saying this *en française.*
44 Though looking at the new blue limbed candy character does, for no apparent reason, call to mind what one of the Beatles® said in *Yellow Submarine®,* "Funny you don't look bluish." In this case, it does.

Petri Dish

This immediately seems more promising. We take a Petri® dish, add a little agar agar and leave the lid off for a few days. Life will find a way. Will it ever. Will it ever. Hoo boy!

As you likely inferred from the previous excursion (p.30), if we take the Petri® dish, add a little agar agar and some viruses, then put on the lid. *Nada.*[45] All the difference in the world!

But this is no biology lab, this is the real world, and we're not dealing with a smallish glass vessel with a tight fitting lid. No. Our "Petri® dish" is an analogy for the wide, wide world. A place full of nutrients that will permit us to cast a wide, wide net and see what grows up between the cracks. This is an analogy rich enough that we can put our bare feet into it—like warm mud—and wiggle our allegorical toes and rejoice. Ooooooh! Aaaaaah!

We should also note that this glass vessel *is* a *Petri*® dish, not a petri dish. [Credit where due.] Julius Richard Petri® was a successful researcher and physician, but few of us would remember him if not for his clever invention of a thing to grow things in. Thus we owe him the honor of capitalization. Like Margot Chafing® with her thing to put hot tuna casserole in, or Leonard Deep® with his pizza pan, or Elmore Satellite® ... but I sense that you think I'm making things up.

These days, of course, the concept of a Petri® dish has grown far beyond the biology lab, assuming an allegorical stance somewhere on the order of a "hotbed," though with somewhat more subtlety.

While pre-revolutionary France was a hotbed (*foyer*[46]) one might say that debates amongst the *philosophes*[47] constituted a *Petri*® dish. Or, say, college campuses in the late 1960s constituted a hotbed of political fervor, while Timothy Leary's explorations were the *Petri*® dish. Or, I don't know, maybe QAnon® comprises the hotbed of current right-wing insanity and Rudi Giuliani's brain is the *Petri*® dish. (No telling what's growing there, but it looks kinda slimy. Def gotta keep a lid on that mess.)

---

45 First use of *español* in the current volume!
46 *En française!*
47 Ditto. *"Idem" en française.*

So, we're dealing with one and not the other. Okay?

Just now Olivia Turnbull is shin-deep in warm mud and she's happily wiggling her toes. [Doesn't that make you want to wiggle yours? I did just now—wiggle I mean, not "want"—an unconscious reaction to composing that sentence. We are all Pavlov® dogs when you come right down to it. Drooling our way through the ding-dongs of life.]

But this little adventure doesn't involve Olivia so we'll just leave her there, singing a wordless song to herself. "La, la, la-la, la." [Wiggle, wiggle.]

Nancy Keyler is a whole nuther ball of wax—no fan of warm mud—but, as they say, "It takes all kinds." [I suspect this is for lack of experience. Yo, Nance? Don't knock it if you haven't ...]

In any event, now that we've caught up with Ms. Keyler, we're ready to crank the old story motor and see what emerges.

Keyler is a grad student and works part time as a lab assistant for Professor Melanie Claymore. I'm sure your immediate guess was that we were headed back to *Petri*® land, but as luck would have it the Professor is a chemist, not a biologist, and the lab work Nance helps with involves catalysts, not, say, nematocysts. [Which, I note, is a "more fun" word. Read it again if you like.]

Nance is somewhat, more or less, rather I'd say, a dedicated, yes dedicated, Bunsen burner[48] aficionado than a Petri-phile. ["Nematocyst," repeated here for "more fun!"]

However, inorganic chemistry is kind of a square peg to fit into the round hole of our "That's Life" rubric, given that it doesn't deal directly with living matter, so we'll just have to follow[49] this young woman home. [Which sounds a little creepy, but don't worry. Nothing untoward will occur.] [Who do you think I am, anyway?]

So, we're walking down University Heights to W.T. Weaver, then over past the Botanical Gardens ("Bo-tan," per locals), to Broadway, hanging back a little so Nance doesn't notice we're on her tail. I mean, no, we're not "on her tail" which, again, would sound kind of creepy. We're just trailing her.

Now up North Street—which, if you ask me, is a pretty lame name for a street, but nobody asked—and then into a side door of a basement apartment—no surprise there, given a grad student budget in the current housing market.

---

48 Invented by Robert Bunsen® at the University of Heidelberg®, in 1854.
49 She walks to the university, making this pretty easy.

Now she's closed the door behind her.
Poop.
Ah, but there's a window!

...

Dare we?

...

[I dunno. This kind of veers toward the creepy again, doesn't it?]
But if we don't, won't the story kind of peter out?

...

While we consider our options, isn't that an interesting turn of phrase? "Peter out." I mean. Obviously, we English speakers know what it "means," but why does it "mean" that?

Traipsing down the etymological Yellow Brick Road®, I found speculative references to St. Peter® being "the rock" that Jesus® supposedly thought to build a church upon, somehow connected to mining and the diminishment of reward at the end of a mineral seam, and then in some way referenced *en française* [which I clearly favor] as *"péter dans la main."*

This phrase Google® translates as "fart in the hand," which, one supposes, is sort of what happens when a story "peters out." Odd, if aromatic.

In the hand? Whatever.

...

Where was I? Oh, the window. Right. Well. If it were just me, I'd be willing to let it go. I mean, I'm not the sort to demand that every story resolve. But it isn't *just* me. It involves you, the reader. You're almost one thousand words into this bit of mischief and if I were to simply walk away ... it would seem s<u>o</u> wrong.

So, here goes.

I ease up, crouched low, fortunately behind a bush so no passers-by will be likely to spot me, and, holding my breath, because if I'm caught doing this it would be personally mortifying, with or without an arrest and the ensuing arrest record, which I *do not need* at this late date, yet, to tell the truth—which I try to do, mostly—just a little titillated, imagining what I might see when I peek, (nudity—or partial undress anyway?)—having what allure it entrains, and notwithstanding the assurance I offered somewhere upslope that this wasn't going to get creepy,[50] then pulling myself up, fingers on brick, eyes just above the sill, peering through the glass.

---

50 Or is this paragraph "creepy" in and of itself?

Curtains.

[Continued from page 196. Whew! Glad I found a blank space.]

At lunch time Jeannette took her salad and a bottle of water to a park bench outside. The rain had moved through overnight and the day was clear and warming. Sitting there in the spring-like weather she noticed an earthworm, evidently washed out of house and home, struggling to cross the driveway. She put down her meal and walked over to it.

"You're gonna get squashed little girl/boy."[400]

She picked it up—it writhed a bit, and carried it to the edge of the woods behind the office and tucked into the loamy soil. "There you go."

Returning to her bench she mulled a bit more trying to puzzle out whether there were any conditions under which: {This statement is true} might not be. She decided that was pretty clearly impossible. Bingo!

General Rule #20: "{This statement is true} is true!"[401]

---

400. Well, we made it! 400! And maybe not the most important footnote in the world. But isn't it sweet the way Jeannette talked to the worm?
401. Okay, not the "best" General Rule, but one that's very hard to argue with.

Warm Mud

The previous, having, in point of fact, "petered out," perhaps we would have been dollars ahead sticking with Olivia. I mean, wiggling one's toes in warm mud is pretty much the cat's pajamas.[51] She certainly seemed to be enjoying herself. But how did she come to be there, shin-deep in ooze? This isn't something most of us would happen into, say, around the house. (Here I may be making an unwarranted assumption. I haven't been in *all that many* houses over the years ... who knows?)

One could imagine that this nice young woman[52] placed a largish enamelware pot—say, one her Mom used in the fall for canning tomatoes—on the stove and filled it halfway with loam and enough water to make it sort of soupy, then turned on the heat and sat atop the refrigerator so she could put her feet ... but, no, that's ridiculous. No one, not even Olivia, would do that.[53]

I know you're thinking that it's the refrigerator part that is beyond the pale and that she could have heated the mud on the stove, then put it on the floor and sat in a kitchen chair to savor the muck. But no. She much prefers her warm wiggles *au naturelle.*[54]

So, where in heck is she? Well, by gosh, she is in Hot Springs, North Carolina!

Most visitors there pay some cash and lounge in hot tubs, which is a pleasant but sort of mechanical experience, with jets that massage whatever part of your anatomy you choose to expose to the stream. But there *is* an alternative.[55] (!)

---

51 This is sometimes used in reference to the pelt of a cat, generally large: i.e. leopard, tiger or lion. This is not my meaning and I'm a bit put out if you thought as much.
52 Writer's tip: good to insert some adjectives to fill in the picture of a protagonist, to help readers identify.
53 She's not just "nice," she's reasonably rational.
54 *En française* and in the *feminine* case, for gender accuracy.
55 Actually there are two alternatives that come to mind. There's the one following footnote #55, and there's the one outside of Tucson. The cool thing about the Tucson alternative is that, at night, you can sit in a hot tub and look down at the sparkling lights of the city, like a what, a galaxy viewed through the Kitt Peak® telescope down south of town? But, the downside is that the state of Arizona is notably dry. The water

If you go just downriver from the hot tub operation the outflow from the natural hot spring runs into the French Broad River and the mud is gloriously warm. This, we now learn, is where Olivia wiggles.

Likely you're wondering why I mentioned Olivia in the first place. Sure, she's "nice," and she likes to wiggle her toes in warm mud ... but ... what?

Well, for one thing, she's a *friend* of Nancy Keyler's. [See? There are no coincidences here.] Furthermore, while she quite enjoys the wiggling and the warmth, she's conducting research. It isn't all *fun and games* with Ms. Turnbull. [Wiggle-wiggle.] As she and Nance and their respective "others"[56] have rafted downstream from Section 9, in Walnut, Liv has been collecting mud samples at the outflow of tributary streams.

Note: I've just realized I may have misinformed you on page 16, regarding boustrophedon composition. I feel I should offer this (potential) correction immediately, rather than let you continue with what may very well be a wrong-headed interpretation. You see, I don't read Ancient Greek Etruscan, and to be quite honest[57] with you, I don't read Modern Greek either.

> That means that she writes left to right on the first line and right to
> a across plow a pulling ox an of manner the in second the on left
> field, then turning at the end of a row. The term is drawn from the
> as" meaning—"turn" ,or *strophe* and ,"ox" or *bous* Greek Ancient
> the ox turns." This pattern was used in Ancient Greek Etruscan and
> ,writers English for unusual pretty is It .languages other few a
> which is why I labeled her (i.e.: Carol) "quirky." I dare say you've not

---

in the tub you inhabit there is heavily chlorinated like the contents of any public swimming pool, because they are hardly going to waste precious water by draining and refilling between customers. (With the heat the odor is a bit overwhelming.) (Wine helps.) The North Carolina Hot Springs water is replaced after each patron or group thereof. Just plain old natural hot water. [Actually, these are simply the two alternatives that sprang up in my memory. There are, obviously, hot tubs all over the place, and hot springs, and hot rods, and hot tamales, and hot tips and hot dates—some of which, we here note—land in hot tubs. Ooo la la! The thing about the Tucson alternative is that it doesn't involve mud. The substrate is dry as a bone. So, I think I might have misled you, and now this footnote has dragged on overlong, so we'll just leave it at that.

56 I hesitate to confuse you with more names.
57 One of my sterling qualities, or so I like to think.

and new something learned you've now But .before it into run likely fascinating, *non?*

Another Note: I ran the first 19 words in the above paragraph through Google Translate®. I think we can agree that it is impossible for most of us to know which direction the words are proceeding in Greek.[58]

Αυτό σημαίνει ότι γράφει από αριστερά προς τα δεξιά στην πρώτη γραμμή και από δεξιά προς τα αριστερά στη δεύτερη[59]

But we've drifted as now have our foursome. Soon they'll be at the Paint Creek takeout and their fine adventure on the ancient French Broad will come to an end. But not Liv's project. No, no! Collecting the samples is only the beginning!

On Monday morning she will begin analysis of her samples!

That oughta be a "thrill a minute" thing, right?

Yeah. Righteo.

Liv is going to put a carefully measured portion of each sample in a test tube and warm it over a Bunsen® burner[60] to drive out the moisture. She will position the tube such that it is warmed, not fried.[61] Also we could observe that she adjusts the flame to its lowest level. All investigative data will be carefully noted in a spreadsheet on her MacBook®.

[This is getting so exciting that I can hardly catch my breath. I mean, she is *warming* her mud!]

Another portion of each sample will be chemically assayed in its moist state and still a third bit of each will be dropped in a puddle of agar agar in Petri dishes! I could just sit here and stare waiting to see what grows!

But I get the sense that some of you readers are less scientifically inclined, so ... maybe it's time for one of those steamy sex scenes for which your author is justifiably famous.

Let's see. After the rafting, when Liv and her unnamed companion arrived home they showered! Naked! [Obviously.} Together! Can't you just imagine? Whooey!

---

58 Assuming "most of us " don't speak Greek.
59 First use of Ελληνικά in the current volume!
60 See page 32.
61 Reminding us for no obvious reason of Bond's "shaken not stirred," or was it the opposite?

Before You Die

Like most people Jeremy Fischer has a bucket list, a compilation of things he'd like to get around to before he can't. Not everyone has an explicit menu, like, say, Angela, in the <u>not to be missed</u> story "Angie's lists."[62] But we all have at least a notion regarding things we hope to have or do or see or experience ahead of the final punt of the dinner pail.

Some days the priorities get rearranged, of course. Even if topping Everest is one of your "must-dos," on any given morning a second cup of coffee might be a more immediate concern.

In any event, Jeremy's bucket is topped by this simple overarching goal: He wants to winnow. All of it. To the "one thing" that will totally "do it" for him. Winnow, winnow, winnow.

"Why?" [I hear you thinking.]

Well, Jeremy has reached the age where our brains finally congeal and rational thought takes hold. Scientists suggest that this is somewhere in the mid-twenties, but there's a good reason the much-heralded Founders® stipulated 35 as a requirement for the presidency, and I suspect they'd have set the bar higher if life-expectancy hadn't generally been so very low back then. You mostly want your president to finish his (or her) term. [Mostly.] Our boy is in his mid-forties.

What he's come to understand is that at any given moment a jet engine could fall off a plane, a Chinese Long March 5B® rocket could leave orbit, an asteroid could come screeching in, or a chunk of steak could get caught in his wind-pipe with no one on hand to maneuver a Heimlich®. His little adventure could be ended in a heartbeat (or lack thereof.[63]) So, it's come to this: what does he most want to do before that turbojet plops on his noggin?

Where to start?

Narrowing one's choices amounts to a conceptual diet, does

---

62 In the memorable collection *Fifty Wheys to Love Your Liver,* Brave Ulysses Books, 2018. As indicated, Angela has multiples.

63 Per Art Garfunkel, "Endings always come at last, endings always come too fast, they come too fast and they pass too slow, I love you and that's all I know.[1]" "All I Know," *Garfunkel,* 1988. Of course, an ending involving a turbojet would not necessarily "pass too slow."
   1. Footnote to a footnote? This is totally true.

it not? This brings us to General Rule #2[64]: "If you want to provide the tools to engineer a successful diet, you need a menu and a shopping list." Impulse buys <u>must</u> be avoided, no matter how good those Dove Bars® or Lay's® potato chips look while you're cruising down the aisle.

So Jeremy came up with three headings after he read "Angie's lists," which made him realize that writing things down was a fine idea.[65] To have. To see. To do.

The first category was simplicity itself. He's not particularly acquisitive and he already has pretty much everything he might want. Ongoing it comes down to food and fuel and an occasional item of clothing, together with replacements for things that break down. Phone, laptop, printer, coffee maker, toothbrush, floss ... that sort of thing. Oh, and eventually another vehicle ... the ephemera of life. No metaphorical "Dove Bars®" in that batch.

To see? There are always the biggies: Grand Canyon, the Egyptian pyramids, the Mara Masai, Machu Picchu, the Louvre®, Hawaii, Alaska, Hudson Bay, the Great Barrier Reef, Graceland® and the other side of the mountain.[66] Those, of course, also involve doing, but the "doing" is principally a matter of getting there. So he'll set that category aside for the nonce.

To do? This is the toughie for at least two reasons.

First off, as noted upslope, Jeremy's brain is fully formed and he's self-aware enough to know that he can't possibly "do it all." That engenders humility, which is one of the most useful realizations in a human life. *Everything* takes longer than we tend to expect and even in the best of circumstances things don't always work out. Also, no matter what you felt at age 16, you aren't invincible and you won't be here very long.[67]

Poof!

Bringing us to the second matter. How to rank the big to-dos? In some ways getting a good night's sleep should be right up

---

64 Amazing! Only on page 39 and we have a second General Rule!
65 I'm sure that story had the same effect on you. Recall that Angela was obsessive enough about lists that she often added things she'd already done so she could have more of them checked off. Laundry√. Call mom√. Go to a Pink Floyd® concert in the rain√. (You really need to read *that* story if you've skipped it.
66 "To see what he could see, to see what he could see!"
67 Your author is looking back from 71 at the moment, and it has gone by way too fast, IMHO. <u>Way too fast.</u>

there, oughtn't it?[68] A lack thereof leaves a soul feeling pretty ragged. But it isn't the sort of thing most people would think of as "bucket-list" material unless they are plagued by insomnia.

What you probably wouldn't guess is that one thing our boy has had in mind ever since he folded his first paper airplane—back in grade-school—is the possibility of building and flying his own real-life flying machine. That has seemed like such a very cool idea! Even if he just used a kit, though "just" is a relative sort of descriptor. One person's "just" in this context could easily be a "Really? You built an airplane from a kit? You are so freaking amazing!"[69]

But then Jeremy read this next sentence and decided against the idea.

A friend of your author who was a HUGE aero-motor enthusiast told him (your author, if that's not clear) about an acquaintance in Idaho who had put together a kit and crashed and died on his first flight.

You can see where that would dampen enthusiasm.

Another "do" on his listicle is to complete a *New York Times®* Sunday crossword puzzle in ink. He'd heard, back in the 90s, that then-prez Bill Clinton® routinely accomplished that, and Jeremy took it as a sort of maxi-personal challenge. Kind of an "anything he can do I can do better" sort of thing. But your author knows[70] that such a feat is hard enough in pencil, with a large eraser at hand. Also, one must entertain deep suspicion[71] that this "factoid" is the product of campaign manager rumor-mongering intended to make the ink-stained candidate appear super-smart.

Is there an un-doctored video of the stunt? I don't think so.

---

68 This is much on your author's mind just now. An arthritic left knee has kept me awake in the wee hours in recent weeks, ibuprofen or no. For a person who habitually rises at 3:30 a.m., pain at midnight is not high on the list of preferences. But I see that I'm interjecting "me."
69 Reminding your author of a fairly singular experience he had back in his twenties, as a mason, in New Hampshire. His employer called the crew to a residential address where we found the block basement wall at the rear of the house had been demolished. What happened? Earthquake? Explosion? Nope. The owner had built an airplane from a kit in his basement and had to tear out the wall to extricate it. Hard to say if that was stupid or ballsy.
70 I know, I know, this isn't supposed to be "all about me." Whatever.
71 I certainly do.

Meanwhile, Clinton was obsessed with a two-letter word,[72] and we who attempt to create[73] crosswords and sell them to *NYT®* know that two-letter words are <u>*not permitted.*</u> So why pull that out in court? (I mean <u>that</u> "argument" not "that" that. You don't want to see "that that" in court.) Right? You have to know it isn't going to fly, at least in public opinion.[74] But public figures caught with their "pants down"[75] are given to wide stretches of their legal imaginations.

Where were we?

Oh, 19 across, "Friend of a 38 down."

That'll stump Bill.

But back to Jeremy. He's pretty deep. He'd so totally like to answer the *Riddle of the Sphinx*. I mean, we all know the <u>answer,</u> right? But he wants to be there. In front of her. And answer correctly. And find out what happens next.

I mean, getting eaten if you fail is one thing, but what happens if you don't? That's the interesting part.

Let's see, what else?

I guess he's winnowed.

Egypt here he comes!

---

72 "It depends on what the meaning of the word 'is' is. If the—if he—if 'is' means is and never has been, that is not—that is one thing. If it means there is none, that was a completely true statement. ... Now, if someone had asked me on that day, are you having any kind of sexual relations with Ms. Lewinsky, that is, asked me a question in the present tense, I would have said no. And it would have been completely true."
—Clinton's Grand Jury testimony Aug. 17, 1998.
 (Parse much?)

73 Guilty.

74 To be clear we are talking about flight-type "fly" and not "that" fly which may have figured in the "is" thing. He should have kept "that" that inside the fly.

75 And why, pray tell (as the expression has it) do so many elected officials have their "pants down?"

Half-life

We're all deeply familiar with the concept of radioactive half-lives, but what about that other sort? Hmm? The number for cesium^{137} or uranium^{238} is easy enough to calculate, (we can all do it in our sleep, right?), but what of our own? You see the problem? You can't know where the half-way point is until you hit the finish line and then ... well, it's a little late. Possibly that's why one's life is said to pass before one's eyes in a near-death situation: a scramble to discern the particulars of hump day.

When, exactly, did the downhill run begin?

As a for-instance, I've lived in North Carolina for more than half of my life *so far,* but that doesn't tell me where the middle was, if, as seems likely, I've passed the center line. Though, who knows? I'm only 71. Maybe I haven't hit half-time? It's a puzzle.

Then too there's the half-life of an earthworm. I was told by someone in my young youth that if you cut an earthworm in two, one half or the other (or both?) will regenerate. I was and am skeptical. Earthworms, which I inevitably sever while digging in the compost bin, do not appear thrilled and my expectation is that neither half survives. I could, of course, be wrong.

Flatworms. You know, planaria? They can and do, even if you cut them into more than two pieces. Each section can regenerate a whole critter, much like the chopped up broom in the Disney® version of the *Sorcerer's Apprentice®*. In all likelihood some—or several—doctoral candidates have carved planaria into smaller and smaller pieces in order to discern the minimus.[76] This, though, makes me wonder about the mind-set of biologists who spend their time cutting up flatworms. Seems half a bubble out of plumb to me.[77]

None of which bears directly on the story at hand.

Banjo Blakeslee is not one to dwell on half-lives, radioactive or otherwise, so how the heck did he end up here?[78] Well, for one thing, Banjo has spent half his life (to date) adjusting claims. Or,

---

76 A single cell? Maybe we should investigate.
77 Notwithstanding the query suggested in Footnote 76.
78 Am thinking Heisenberg. We don't know Banjo's mass or location or speed or anything else of much use. But Heisenberg wouldn't be surprised. Banjo appeared. Poof!

for we who pay for insurance rather than working for insurers, he spends that time *reducing* claims. Even halving them! If he were inclined to adjust them upward he'd be out of a job in a New York minute.[79] (I guess somebody has to do it in order to keep wealth bubbling up to the top.)

But he must have some redeeming characteristics, right? Don't we all?

He may, but I don't know what they might be, so let's move along.

Jill[80] Steenbergen met Banjo once in the unfortunate circumstance of filing a claim, but she's gotten over it. Jill is a Montessori[81] teacher, and a good one. The whole drill there is "no-drill." Teachers let students explore the world and lead the way into things they want to learn. Unfortunately (for the students) her school, like most Montessori operations, ends at age six, and the bright, self-directed tykes mostly end up regimented into highly structured regimens. That must be a total shocker.

At age 12 they'll have spent half their little lives being free, and at 18, only one third ... you do the math.

Jill is a pretty tolerant sort, as you might well imagine. Within the range of children's safety she'll go with their flow. For instance, when Jasper (age 5-1/2) found an earthworm in the playground he wanted to cut it in half to see if it would grow a new tail (or head?).

"Why do you think that would happen?"
"My big brother said it would."
"Do you think it would hurt the worm?"
"I don't know."
"Do you know how they eat?"
"They do?"
"Yes. See this end? That's the head."
"The head?"
"And there's a little tiny mouth."
"A mouth?"
"Maybe we could put it in the terrarium and see if we can see it eating." (See how cleverly Jill has redirected the child?)

"Okay. Then can we cut it in half?"

---

79 Actually a "New Haven" minute, but that is not an "idiom."
80 A girl named Jill was my first puppy crush. FWIW.
81 I was going to insert a trademark® here, but I learned that the name isn't trademarked. I'm keen on accuracy.

Down Among The Ruins

How well we recall Ned Fowler the professor who landed *way* down among the ruins and lost half a leg to boot![82] Lucky fellow. Those were the days my friend! Those were the days.

But the present little adventure involves a different sort of ruin (i.e., not Olmec®[83]) and, get this, a different sort of down! [All I can say is "Oh, goody!"]

As I write this morning Russia is a bit over three months into turning much of Ukraine into ruins, so we could probably find a setting there if we liked, but ancient ruins have the distinct advantage that any dead bodies that were strewn around are already back to dust. Ukraine, just now, is beyond gruesome. And, of course, weapons from the E.U., U.K. and U.S. are doing their share.

On the plus side, Kurt Vonnegut® advised authors that they had to kill one or more characters in order to make fiction work. Not clear if my tax dollars give me a claim in that regard.

Let's see. We've done Olmec®. Two stories upslope Jeremy was headed for Egypt. In a not-to-be-missed love story, "Dee Minimus," we followed Dee into the recesses of a cliff dwelling in Arizona up on the Mogollon Rim.[84] Oh, and we covered Greek and Roman leftovers in *Lucky Breaks*[85] as well. Inca? No. We did up Inca in "Tummy Tuck."[86] Viking? Nope. Jazzy went to *L'anse aux Meadows* in "Wrecked."[87] Aztec? Went there with that "volunteer" virgin destined for heart-rending sacrifice in "Cutting Loose."[88]

What we seem to be looking for is a new ruin, but a ruin that's older than, say, Mariupol, which has only been wrecked in

---

82 In the first gripping tale in *Lucky Breaks,* Brave Ulysses Books, 2022.
83 It is a fascinating fact that not all ruins are Olmec®! Is it not?
84 In the sterling collection *Seize You on the Dark Side of the Moo,* (BUB, 2019) in which she enjoyed a hot and heavy with a paleoneotomologist, which is a real thing.
85 Notice how I'm weaving references to other works in my "storied" output? This is done as a lesson for other writers. Untold is unsold!
86 The story about the nudist travel agent and her wealthy clients in *Waist Not, Want Knot,* BUB, 2020.
87 Also in *Lucky Breaks.*
88 A thriller found in *Cede Catalog,* BUB, 2021

recent weeks. That is to say, a ruin new to our accumulation of something like 200 (count em!) short stories, but actually, or metaphorically, lost in the sands of time. And also ... near water.

It *must* be near water.

Oh, I've got it! That ancient French chapel, sans roof, in the *Loire* valley. How well I recall! That's where we now discover Bertie and Tara.[89] They've been on a cycling tour of the *campagne française* for about a week and now they have stopped in mid-afternoon for a snack—a bit of runny cheese, some crackers and, *naturellement du vin*.[90]

They're quite taken by the scenery. Roses are blooming in profusion—grown over stuccoed walls. Fields are orange with poppies and others golden with oil-seed sunflowers. Church spires and *château* bespeak centuries of cultured wealth oppressing ill clothed, under-fed peasantry. And now this ruin, a testament to both stone mason skills and the ravages of fire and time. The notches where roof beams were once cradled today house birds' nests. Saplings and weeds have grown out of the tiled pavement. It is truly a ruin among ruins! It *fires* the imagination!

Our couple would have been enjoying soaring ideas even without wine going a bit to their heads, but now the afternoon has become fabulous! They are hand holding and laughing, stealing an occasional kiss, and feeling fully carefree.

Just across the way there is a pond as well, which adds the sort of charm that only a limpid body of water can provide. And look! A flock of white ducks![91]

[Tara is an amateur naturalist and happens to know a thing or two about *Anas platyrhynchos*.] "Honey, did you know that practically all white ducks are descended from mallards?"

"I thought all mallards had green heads, at least the males."

"That was bred out of them for some reason."

"Oh."[92]

The birds, evidently accustomed to begging from tourists are out of the *étang*[93] now,and are waddling toward the couple,

---

89 Yes they are lovers, but at the moment in question they are fully clothed, so calm down.
90 Five French words in one paragraph! National Book Award® here we come!
91 Providing us with the titular down, assuming the waterfowl cross the road to join the two picnickers.
92 Adding "interesting" dialogue makes a story so much more exciting!
93 Pond *en français,* this being a puddle *français.*

quacking all the way, eliciting more laughter from our pair who are soon crumbling crackers for the beggars.

"They are so funny!"[94]

Now that we have inserted the requisite "down" we can move along with our story. [As the old joke has it: "You can't get down off an elephant."]

Tara is from just down[95] the road which is how I happen to know her. She's currently the manager of a women's clothing boutique down[96]town, but she was able to claim a two week vacay thanks to having a reliable assistant.

Cathy is well able to handle the business while Tara's away because they've worked together for almost a decade. While the two share competency in their trade they are in many ways quite different. *The assistant, for just one telling example, doesn't know a thing about ducks!* Also, you wouldn't guess it just to look at them, but *Tara doesn't play the oboe!*

Cathy is a jazz oboist, which is about as rare a bird as you'll encounter in this or any life, white mallard or no. On weekend nights you'll find her *getting down* with a bass player, a drummer and a scat singer at one of the clubs over in the Arts district which is where the actual story part of this story takes place.

To wit:

One night when Cathy was playing, Bertie and Tara were there, enjoying the music together with some runny cheese and wine when two wait-staffers, both former cops, pulled a good waiter/bad waiter on them.[97]

It was hilarious!

---

94 This might have been said by either participant.
95 Third down and goal to go! (Previous involved ducks and elephants if you are skipping around.)
96 Fourth and goal? Will we find another?
97 To get a sense of why this would be such a scream you'd do well to read "Busted²" in *Lucky Breaks,* in which officers Newsome and Pronke take turns, that is "trading roles," with the good cop/bad cop routine, thoroughly confusing their suspects. "Weren't you the bad cop last time?" one perp queries. Heh heh. Also check out "Upper crust" on page 97 in the current volume.

Time After Time

[That last go-round was rather heavily laden with self-promotion. I'll steer past that for the present.]

Burr Brubaker is our protagonist (or victim) this time around. He's tallish.[98] Also, he works in a bank.

I realize that this immediately suggests that he's a clerk, or a teller, or an account manager of some kind, dealing with deposits and withdrawals and the sort of careful record keeping that checking and saving and certificates of deposit (CDs) and IRAs and loans and payment plans and so on and so forth[99] entail. But no.

Burr works in a sperm bank, which, obviously enough, requires deposits, and I guess "withdrawals", but, unlike the financial type, involves cryogenics along with other details that we really don't want to go into here. [We're aiming for a general audience.]

How well we recall the two young women whose DNA tests revealed that they shared ... oh, sorry. I almost ... so, nevermind.

When Burr was driving home the other day he heard a story on the radio that really piqued his interest. That doctor who pretended to be artificially inseminating women with semen from anonymous donors, but was actually using his own? [Talk about "time after time."] That one? He was convicted. [The upside being that he has lots and lots of kids who might well visit him in prison. Or who might be imprisoned *with* him. As in the case of the mattress people, who would know?[100]]

Oh, by-the-by, Burr is in management, not "administration," so he's in no position to do the same if he wanted to. Which he does not. He's one of our "good eggs." This suggests, by the way, General Rule #3. "As we go through life, time after time we are likely to enjoy more reliable results when we deal with good eggs." [101]

But the radio report did get Burr to thinking, which is as

---

98 To you writers out there, take note! Readers like to know something about your characters!
99 My grandfather used this phrase a lot. A *whole* lot.
100 See page 13 and so on and so forth. (Ding! 100 footnotes!)
101 You can quote me on this. Also true of *in vitro* fertilization.

good a reason to listen to NPR® as one can imagine. (Or only?)

Here's the thing: "Thoughts just emerge, you don't think them *before* you think them."[102]

This sounds simple enough but it is a rabbit-hole of the first order. It takes us right down the bunny tunnel to matters of free will and the urgent matter of "who's in charge here?" Do we decide or are the decisions already made? [In wider stretches of the imagination, are we a computer simulation ginned up by an adolescent mattress-person on the planet Serta® (or Sealy®?) orbiting *Alpha Centauri?*]

Take any decision you make and try to work backward to see the cocoon (or cave) it flew out of and you very quickly realize that your entire life has pretty clearly been a series of Russian nesting dolls going all the way back. This because of that, that because of the other, the other contingent on what seemed like a good idea at the moment. Oh boy. "That which seemed like a good idea."[103] Road to hell and all. Even the fact of your "being" isn't something you chose. You popped out of Mom, and that entails another whole series of Russian doll incidents ranging back to either: 1) the first chimpanzee who could ... but, no, that opens up another product line of furry figurines[104]; or 2) Eve and that portentous apple.

If everything depends on "initial conditions" and then simply flows, where does "free will" come in?

So we can well imagine Burr having what NPR® refers to as a "driveway moment"—those attentive and perhaps introspective, or in other cases "outro-spective," times you leave the car running —contributing unnecessary carbon to the climate crisis—in order to hear the end of a story.

Everything emanates from pre-existing conditions. We like to think we could choose differently but obviously that other choice rolls down the chute from the same gumball machine as

---

102 Quoting Sam Harris® as heard on a Lex Fridman® podcast.
103 The source of all travail. And where did *that* idea come from?
104 Per Oliver Sacks®, in *The New Yorker*®, April 27, 2015, "(Apes and monkeys, like children, though clearly intelligent and capable of forethought and planning are relatively lacking in frontal lobes, and tend to do the first thing that occurs to them, rather than pausing to reflect. Such impulsivity can be striking in patients with frontal-lobe damage.)" Yeah, well, Mr. Sacks, This sounds so deep, but, when those of us without "frontal-lobe damage" pause to "reflect" we still do the thing that occurs to us. First or whatever.

the one we "decided" against. We enjoy jokes like the one that poses the conundrum: "Should I walk to work or take lunch?"[105] But in sober moments we know the decision was made long ago. It's no wonder so many people believe in original sin, but it's hilarious to notice that those same people mostly think it can be undone. Nope. That horse left the barn a long time ago.

So. After Burr turns off the engine he sits quietly for a bit, thinking about everything in the last five paragraphs and asks himself the obvious question. "Then my choices don't matter?"

Ah, Burr, Burr. All the men and women may merely be players, but we still have to perform our parts. The show goes on. The show goes on. It *all* matters.

---

105 Oh that one cracks me up!

Teach a ~~man~~ person to fish

I nearly fell into that trap. It isn't just men who angle, right? And then the first part of that old saw regarding the giving of fish? Well, in my experience, and not to be sexist, if you give a man a fish he'll probably throw it in a frying pan, maybe with some butter, whereas, again based on my experience, if you give a woman a fish she's more than likely going to season it in interesting ways, perhaps douse it with lemon juice or wine, perhaps tarragon vinegar, maybe something zingy like red pepper oil, plus herbs and spices, and then bake it, or perhaps bread it with flavored crumbs of some Indo-European variety.

This is why, when I'm in fish-giving mode, I give fish to women and hope I'll be invited to dinner.

But as for the teaching part, I have my Mom to thank. [See cover photo.] Dad was only interested in smelt. Back in my youth the springtime smelt run in Lake Michigan was beyond astonishing. You could almost walk on them, there were so many. Just stand on the pier after dark and dip your net and you'd have a bucket-full in no time. Tasty? Oh my, yes.

Some folks filled pick-up truck beds for freezing and, one supposes, sale.

These days predator fish in the Great Lakes® have bounced back from their mid-century nadir and there are reportedly fewer smelt for the smelters, which is just as well since the little fish have been found to accumulate industrial waste toxins to the point that medical folk advise eating no more than one serving per month. A pick-up load would last a lifetime at that rate.

This takes me back to my earliest chicken-with-its-head-cut-off memory.[106] When we were preparing the smelt for frying (Dad was in charge. See the third sentence up top) the first step was popping off the head. I discovered that if I did that and dropped the fish back in the bucket ... it kept on swimming! What? (It would be decades before I actually witnessed a chicken performing the same stunt.) (Running, not swimming.)

Outside of that one night each spring Dad had absolutely no use for "fishing" and, honestly, that wasn't exactly "fishing." It

---

106 Coupled with the worm thing two stories back, this makes me wonder why, in a collection I've labeled "That's Life" I am busily dissevering.

was basically "shooting fish in a barrel," though that expression makes approximately no sense.

Why are the fish in a barrel? Why would you need to shoot them if they were already captive? Has anyone ever actually done this? Or seen anyone doing so? Or wanted to? Historically the only references I've ever seen to the presence of cold-blooded aquatic vertebrates in a cask involved salt, back before ice became readily available for shipment. Not much sense wasting ammunition on a few firkins of pickled pike.

Mom loved to fish year-round, even ice-fishing! She'd take me and my brother to docks, piers, jetties, beaches, frozen lakes and boats. We'd bait and bobber, bottom fish and surf-cast. We went out on party-boats in the Gulf of Mexico and came home with grouper![107] [See front cover! Look at those fish!]

Come to think of it, *she's* the one who taught me to cut worms in half.[108] Her theory was that half a worm was every bit as good for bait as a whole worm and you therefore were doubling your supply. She also taught me to go out pre-dawn with a flashlight to collect night-crawlers.[109]

On the other hand, Mom wasn't much of a reader. That was Dad's thing. So there was a sense of intellectual balance in the homestead. Mom would read maybe half a book all summer. Something fat like James Michener®'s *Hawaii*. Dad would read a book or two each week. Mostly science fiction. [His *Harvard Classics®* may have been more posture than intellectual bent, though he could well have read those before I popped out.]

I'm not sure why I'm telling you all this, other than, perhaps, to set things up for the following thrilling tale.

Kevin's Mom was a fisher-person too. (!)

This little *vignette*,[110] however, is about Kevin's father, who wasn't. Actually, come to think of it, it isn't exactly about him, it's about his brother's wife. His father's brother's wife if that isn't clear. So that makes it about Kevin's aunt by marriage.

Sylvia is a very <u>interesting</u> person. Her sister told me this over coffee a couple of weeks ago.

---

107 There's something appropriate about catching grouper when you're out with a group on a party boat, is there not?
108 Thinking back to page 43, though the intent was not to regrow.
109 This is very likely the reason I habitually wake at 3:30 or 4 a.m. to begin my writing day. Early birds and writers get the worms. Proof of the worms thus corralled is presently in your eager hands.
110 *Française!*

I've known Janese for ages and feel pretty certain she wouldn't try to bamboozle me, except perhaps on April first. So I'm pretty darn certain Sylvia *is* "interesting."

I recall the time Janese and I pulled a couple of tricks on *her* nephew (not Kevin, if that isn't clear) after his wedding.

First we stuffed an old pair of pants and some socks with rags and put it under the happy couple's car so when they came out after the reception they would think there was a body there. Heh heh. But that wasn't the best one. Oh no. No, no, no.

Then Janese and I went to the motel where we'd learned the newlyweds had reserved a room where they were going to spend the first night before heading off on their honeymoon. She was wearing a white dress and I had on a suit and tie so we easily posed as the lately spliced couple. She asked the night clerk for the key-card to "our" suite. Heh heh. He happily complied.

We went upstairs and scoped things out. There was a balcony with wrought iron decorative vertical stanchions extending to the ground level. Oh boy!

We short-sheeted the bed, wrote CONGRATULATIONS! On the bathroom mirror with her lipstick, filled the tub with bubblebath (her idea, not clear why), locked the door and climbed down the ironwork from the balcony. Heh heh.

We learned later that the clerk refused to let the real couple have a key for an hour or more until he could get hold of a manager who demanded the pair produce identification. Heh heh.

Honestly, that whole escapade was Janese's idea and it so amused me that I gave her a fish!

I gave her a fish!

But she didn't invite me to dinner.

Sigh.

It's the little things

Isn't it?

I mean, a bear will get your attention, particularly if you're hiking alone on some subarctic trail and the animal in question is a grizzly,[111] but how often does *that* happen? Fleas on the other hand? They are never singular and they can easily be maddening.

(We'll get to the story part shortly. The following is true. My then-partner and I used to travel for months at a time. Upon returning to our abode with our cats and dog we didn't want to expose them to the resident flea population that we knew would have hatched and lain in wait for the next succulent mammal to wander in. Nor, as organicists, would we bomb the place with pesticides. So we'd leave the cats and dog in the camper, take off our shoes and socks and pants, and wade into the fray. Fleas would mob us. With our legs peppered with little hungries we'd jump in the bathtub and wash them down. Again and again until the coast was clear. It was kind of satisfying. We spared our pets and ourselves a great deal of looming future misery.)

Or arctic, if you're out on the ice and an immense white bruin pops into view. (Again, that's a rarity, given that most of us prefer moderate warmth to blistering cold.) But fleas? They have it way over polar bears. I mean, really. Getting eaten by a big alabaster beast would happen pretty darn fast. Getting eaten by fleas? Interminable. (Strickland Gilliland® gained fame if not fortune by composing what is generally deemed to be the shortest English language poem ever written: "Adam had 'em." If true—and how could we know—one wonders if God made the fleas post-apple as part of the punishment regimen. Exile would have been at least a little more pleasant in their absence.) Having a polar bear attached to your ankle would be a one-and-done. Fleas will go on all summer. Better dead than ... well, I don't have a rhyme here ... "than being progressively lunched on in itchy despair."

---

111 This may be a good moment to quote Annie Dillard®—there being many good moments to quote Dillard, of course. "I have read that in the unlikely event that you are caught in a stare-down with a grizzly bear, the best thing to do is talk to him softly and pleasantly. Your voice is supposed to have a soothing effect." *Pilgrim at Tinker Creek,* p. 202. I think that sounds about right. You go first.

But we have let the fleas divert our attention from the much more important "little things." (As they will.)

There are, in point of fact, things much smaller than fleas which can and do trouble a weary mind. (To rather invert Harmie Smith®'s classic, "Weary trouble on my mind." But we do inversions here at will. We are practically linguistic contortionists!)

So, no—not doing flea here. We're going hypodermic deep.

Wilinda Bates is utterly fascinated by one of the simplest and in its way "smallest" concepts in the magical field of pure mathematics, though its implications are huge.[112] [I bet you already want to get to know her better even though you've only just met!]

Let's see. She lives alone and lives in her head a lot, so her housekeeping is pretty slack. "Cluttered," applies, as does "dusty." But within that frame she's also surprisingly organized. The stacks of reading material are as orderly as books on a library shelf, Dewey decimaled as the dickens.[113] Magazines are sequential by volume, issue and date. In the midst of a conversation she can whip out an article from three years back that addresses precisely your immediate concern. Or hand you a book on the topic.

She's slim.

Her favorite color is Cadet Blue.

Food is a minor concern and her diet is pretty monotonous. I guess she's an "eat to live" vs. "live to eat" sort.

What else?

Um, she's 43. (Literally in her "prime!") (Or one of them.)

And, of course, like all of my favorite make-believe people, she has a cat. Her name is Pomonella.[114]

I know you are waiting with bated breath to learn more! (Or is that "baited?" I'm never quite clear on that. Does the term derive from "abated?" Or is it the sense of hoping to catch something? See worm reference on page 51.[115])

She's been married three times![116]

She was born on August 13th! Her weddings were on

---

112 Talk about deep!
113 Dickens®, of course, has long been Deweyed. Though not his fiction.
114 Like all of the cats in my fiction Po was a real companion of mine, on loan to Wilinda for purposes yet to be revealed. (Po lived to age 23!)
115 Also, we here note, prime, as is this footnote.
116 Another prime! Also, three times divorced.

January 17th, May 27th and September 29th! In 2003, 2011 and 2017, respectively!

Wilinda's ruling passion is for prime numbers, as by now you've surely guessed. As Alec Wilkinson® noted in *A Divine Language*,[117] "Prime numbers are where imaginary mathematics begins." *Imaginary* mathematics! Ooooh!

Her favorites are mostly tetradic primes, that is, those numbers that are prime backward and in a mirror: 11, 101, 1881881 and the like. Sometimes she gets out a pencil and paper and spends hours dividing primes by themselves which she finds relaxing.

1881881/1881881=1, 3/3=1, and etc.

[I'm obviously kidding here. Wilinda would hardly find such amusing. What she actually does is this: she divides primes by primes. Say, 1881881/3. Try it! No, not on your phone or laptop calculator. On paper. Or 1881881/7. Gosh.]

Her least favorite divisor is 2. "It doesn't seem right," she told me. "An even number shouldn't be allowed in. Division of primes by 2 always ends in point 5."

[I'm sure you agree—but that's not where we're going with this exciting tale.]

She is independently wealthy, one reason why she's never fallen into the economic matrimony trap that often keeps women in marriages they'd rather exit—women's wages being what they generally are.

How so? (I hear you thinking.)

She actually invented a better mouse trap!

Now you're probably wondering where you can obtain the same.

You can't.

:-(← Sad face.[118]

Wherefrom, then, her great wealth? (I hear you thinking.) (Keep it up. You're making this story work!)

In the old days an inventor of a handy gizmo would obtain a patent, set up shop, perhaps with an angel investor, and start production. Think fingernail clipper.

I'm pretty sure we can all agree that a modern style fingernail clipper is right up there with mouse traps and flea combs when it comes to making life livable: i.e. it is no "little thing." Up until 1875 when Valentine Fogerty® obtained a U.S. patent for

---

117 Farrar, Straus & Giroux, 2022. (Three names. Are we surprised?)
118 This puts me in the "graphic novel" category for the Book Award®.

something like the nail trimmers we use today, and Hungarian inventor David Gestetner® did the same in the United Kingdom, people used knives or their teeth. (Lacking a knife you'd have to get someone else to bite your toenails, unless you were a contortionist, of course.) Production and sales started directly.

But that was then and this is now.

Under late-stage capitalism a patent is often purchased by a corporation with no intent whatever of actually *making* the gizmo, rather the goal is to prevent *anyone else* from making it. In Wilinda's case there was a bidding war with the winner eventually proffering $3 million.

You see, her design would cost more to manufacture than the old-fashioned spring bar on a block of wood. Market analysts believed the profit margin would be narrow, but feared its availability could disrupt the market. After all, many people think of dead mice as icky and throw the used traps away with rodent attached rather than doing the sane thing—to drop the mouse in the compost pile and reuse the unit. Hers could be cleanly and handily emptied, hence reused. Not a good business plan.

[That, or the things would work so well that house mice would vanish, completely collapsing the lucrative industry.]

Wilinda is a stickler, however, and demanded payment of $61,209 per month for 49.9 months. [She has her standards!]

As for her home rodent control issues, that's where Pomonella comes in. She was a heck of a mouser in life and is the same in her fictional role. Back in the days when Susan and I were wending our peripatetic way around the continent, Po would catch mice at campsites, and naturally enough, around the home place, where mice were as likely to move in during our absence as fleas.[119] The most amazing thing about Po, however—in my view, apart from living to age 23 [23!]—was this.

Living in the woods in those high and far off times, our felines were indoor/outdoor.[120] Po was particularly fond of squirrels. She'd eat them whole, except for their tails and one odd internal organ. (Spleen maybe?)

I thought you'd want to know.

Meanwhile, Wilinda is trying to find the next prime. No small thing.

---

119 And were likely the, or at least "a" source of the fleas. Note this footnote is not prime. (7 x 17) Nor is the next. Sigh.
120 Quiet dirt road, virtually no traffic. Since I moved into the city two decades ago my buddies are strictly indoor.

Born and razed

I don't know about you, but that title troubles me. Where in hell did it come from? Who was it and what happened? I think it will be best to ignore it and move along.

This brings us to General Rule #4: "Titles are not *entitled*." Just saying.

Rob Kincaid, like all the rest of us, was born, and grew up, but he never grew a beard or shaved his head, which is something.[121] He's a reader which is also something and stands him in good stead in my view. However what we want to discuss first here is his work, since the "what do you do" question always seems to be aimed at job info.

As I've mentioned elsewhere, though not in this volume, you can have a lot of giggles with that question if someone asks. You could say, "I exhale," or "I procrastinate," and just leave it at that. "I do the hokey-pokey." Funny, or what?

But here we're being serious and straight-forward. Rob is a potter, up to his elbows in clay all week long. *Un artiste!*[122]

Like most artists he is just bursting with creative spirit and like most potters he makes most of his income from mugs, some from bowls, a little from plates and virtually nothing from his *chefs-d'œuvre artistiques*.[123] This is somewhat sad, but certainly true. His delightfully imaginative sculptures almost never sell. Ah, well.

He's hardly alone in this, of course: A photographer is far more likely to earn a living shooting wedding pics than street scenes and vistas; A blacksmith or welder from shoeing horses or structural repair than metal yard-art; A high-school basketball ace from coaching the next generation—not playing for the NBA®. Etc.

It's the practical that generally pays. Actually, let's make that General Rule #5. "It's the practical that generally pays."[124]

---

121 I can't emphasize enough the edification one experiences from either of these practices, particularly the latter. So Rob lacks some measure of edification. Shave your head if you doubt me. Do it!
122 We haven't used *française* for a bit. It makes art "artier," *non?*
123 See what I mean? "Artistic masterpieces" sounds so plebian.
124 Two General Rules on one page! Wowza!

It's what happened to Rob yesterday that concerns us here.

He had just finished for the day and had a few dozen[125] new mugs on a drying rack. He'd cleaned his wheel and tools and washed up, feeling reasonably satisfied with what he'd accomplished. [If only every factory-type laborer were as pleased with a day's work!]

Rob strolled from his studio to his little cottage, through a garden in full bloom. [If only every wage-slave in mug manufacture could walk to work! Through a garden, no less!]

When he entered the house, there was Liz, lying on the sofa, reading,[126] seductively dishabille in a gauzy tank top and bikini-style panties—oh, and socks, <u>red socks</u>—but *nothing* else.

[If only every diligent manual worker could come home come evening to such a delightful scene! Red socks!]

"Hi sugar," she said, looking up from the book. "Good day?"

"Went well, hon."

"Did you notice I'm scantily clad?" She batted her eyes. "And seductively draped on our couch?"[127]

"Indeed, indeed! You have me aroused! You arouseth me."

"That was my plan. But I need to finish reading this story first. It's about a nudist who shows up at a fellow's house one day and moves in! Just like *that!* Just wild!"[128]

"Honestly hon, I think scantily clad is sexier than nude. 'Specially when it's you."

"You're sweet."

Just then Rob's phone rang, he pulled it out of his pocket and answered. Liz turned back to her reading.

"Rob here."

We can't hear the voice on the other end of the convo, which is a shame. This would be a hell of a lot more interesting if we had some clue what he is hearing. [Perhaps we could make something up? But I'm loathe. Putting words in peoples' mouths is not really fair, and unlikely to be accurate. Fairness and accuracy in media is my goal, this book being a form of media, though not what most people think when they think "media."]

---

125 When dry, bisqued, glazed, fired again, several hundred dollars worth of merch.

126 One of my books as it happened. *Waist Not, Want Knot.*

127 It looks like we're on the verge of one of the steamy scenes for which I am arguably famous! They are on the verge of a diddle!

128 This is the first story in *Waist Not,* so she has almost 200 pages of humor and insight ahead of her. Lucky woman!

"Really?"
Another long listen here. [Gosh, I wish we could hear —"who, what, where, why, when?"]
"Okay. Will do."
Again. From the "other," a protracted disquisition.
"ASAP, bro. ASAP."

So here we have a dilemma. We can jump ahead and learn that it was, in fact, his brother. John, his *hapless* brother. His ever-failing-to-attend-to-automotive-maintenance-brother. Once again with car trouble and needing a ride. "Right away."

And we have seductive Liz. Ready and willing and evidently eager, certainly "scantily clad." [Also, we should note, this volume has been somewhat shy of "hot'n'steamies." This might be a good juncture. Sex scenes sell!]

So, what?
Rob disrobes. (!) Jumps in the shower. (!) Whence he shaves. (!) [Being razed ...]
He then conjoins with Liz![129] Who quickly becomes even less shabile. [Except for the socks. Red socks are sexy.] Etc. and etc. And even more etc.[130] Much more etc.[131]
[If only every ...]

Post-diddle Liz tells him the rest of the story about Lurlene, the nudist, and Nutter. But that tale's been told already,[132] so we won't go into it now.

A good while later Rob will rescue John, his brother getting somewhat less "lucky" than our potter, but, lucky enough.
Lucky enough.

---

129 My heart is aflutter. They are diddling!
130 Whooey!
131 Can you imagine? I mean ...
132 The title story in *Waist Not, Want Knot* as mentioned in footnote 128.

World enough. And time.

Still panting here. But, to be clear, Elizabeth isn't always scantily clad, and although she's enjoying the book she's been reading,[133] she "has a life." I know her titillating presence on the couch might have made it appear that she lives a "life of leisure," but that is not so. She works for a living and, like Rob, from home. So there's that.

Liz could tell you: "There are, for instance, two hundred and twenty-eight separate and distinct muscles in the head of an ordinary caterpillar."[134] From which you might easily surmise that her work involves the counting of muscles in the heads of bugs.

Or worms. Or larvae.

But no.

That's just something she read three paragraphs up where I quoted Dillard. (As we noted before the preceding amazingly steamy interlude, she's a reader. But that's not her "job.")

What she is is this: a consultant!

Which leaves us wondering. How did a potter get hooked up with a consultant?

Clay work is pretty matter of fact. You wedge, you throw, you turn, you pull up or out, you fire, you glaze, you fire again, and so on and so forth. It is tangible.

Consultancy? Not so much. Words. Opinions. Advice. Maybe good, maybe less so. Results may vary. Oh, the recipient may benefit and—if the advisor is a good talker—*feel* helped, or maybe feel *mollified,* or perhaps feel *better prepared* for the next step in life's little happy-dance, but ... only time will tell.

Did Rob need consulting?

No.

Then what? (I hear you thinking.)

You see, one tool absolutely essential to a professional consultant—and you can take my word on this, since I have met a few over the years—though I haven't actually employed one to date, but who knows? (Maybe? Do you think I need one?) The thing being that I am a keen observer who quickly grasps the "stock in trade" of the worker-bees I meet. <u>Consultancy requires a</u>

---

133 See footnote 125.
134 We can thank Annie Dillard® for this one.

coffee mug.[135] Elizabeth had had one. A favorite. But, like all ceramics must eventually do,[136] it had fallen. To pieces.

[Just outside my front door, adjacent to the astilbes and an azalea, beside the row of impatiens, I have a stoneware graveyard —brightly glazed remnants of cups and plates and vases that have met their inevitable demise, but remain too attractive to consign to the landfill. *"Sic transit gloria mundi."*[137]]

That happened three years ago and Liz needed a new mug. She'd seen Rob's shingle and popped into his studio. The item she selected had his signature exterior texture formed by the trailing of his fingers as the clay turned—four shallow grooves. When she picked it up her fingers fit naturally into them.

"This is beautiful," she offered. "But more than that, it fits my hand perfectly."

Rob's hands were clean at the moment—he was glazing, not throwing at the time—and, being a practical sort[138] he took her hand in his, then placed them both palm-to-palm.

"That explains that," he laughed. "Assuming this mug is for you as versus a gift, when you use it we'll practically be holding hands."

"I wouldn't complain."

"In that case, what are you doing for dinner? There's a new place two blocks from here that I've heard is good. I've been looking for an excuse."

"You're on."

One thing led to another and another and another, moving in, scant cladding[139] and all. But I'll stop here before another hot'n'steamy gives me the flutters.

---

135 I think this qualifies as General Rule #6. "Consultancy requires a coffee mug."
136 She had turned in her office chair while reaching for her phone. Her elbow clipped the cup and down it went. Tile floors are relatively unforgiving when it comes to ceramics and Newtonian physics..
137 We haven't had any Latin for a while.
138 See the eighth graf on the preceding page.
139 No "coyness," which justifies the story title.

Thanks. For the memories.

Or mammaries, for those of us who were fortunate enough to be breast-fed—a nod of gratitude too often overlooked. "How I love ya, how I love ya, my dear old Mamm(ar)y!"

I would venture to guess, however, that few among us actually *remember* that experience. Back when I popped up on the scene nursing was a very private matter for most average Americans, so finding a photo of Mom'n'me *in flagrante delicto*[140] is pretty unlikely and photos are the way most of us capture "memories" of our very young youth.

[Breast feeding still remains controversial as a public practice in some circles, of course, but less so as time flows on.]

Anyone who claims to clearly recall is almost certainly making things up, but as Patsy would ask, "Are we surprised?"

We had a long talk about that several years ago (though, obviously, you have no way of knowing whether that statement is true.) She was painting my deck—I have very little patience with balusters, and she is a pro. (I did the pressure-washing, just to let you know that I'm no slacker. And a good bit of scraping.) She's deft and dab and thorough. No holidays. I mean in the coat of paint. She does "take" holidays, she just doesn't leave them.

This reminds me of the first time I heard that phrase when a carpenter friend named Paul hired me to paint his exterior window trims. Paul had married into money and had begun to hire out work he'd rather not do himself. "No holidays," he'd said in his thick "New Ham-shah" accent.

I'd responded that I hadn't scheduled one and he set me straight. "Paintah's holidays, my man, paintah's holidays."

How does this relate to Patsy and memory? Well, for one thing, when I referenced the concept a couple of inches upslope I immediately recalled Paul, but—here's the thing—I didn't instantly *recall his name.* I pulled up his face, with his handlebar mustache but it took me a few beats to remember his name. I haven't thought about him for many, many decades.

[I now wonder how he's doing. Men, we recall, suffer.[141]]

---

140 I realize that this phrase is somewhat misapplied here, but it's been a full page since we did some Latin. Latin is fun!
141 See page 22 regarding heartache. Though, who knows?

What Patsy was telling me was about something she'd lately read.¹⁴² Memory is pretty shaky. The things we recall most accurately are the things we recall suddenly after a long time. Things we pull up frequently are changed each time we consider them.

So my little vignette regarding Paul is precise right down to his mustache. That *was* his name. He *did* marry into money. [She later dumped him.] I recall also the first time he told me he was dating the woman—who's name I won't use here, though I do now remember it. "She's rich!" he'd said. "Oh," I said—that never having been one of my criteria regarding matters of the heart. "Really, really rich!¹⁴³ I'm going to marry her!" ["Oh," I said, thinking, "This isn't going to work."] [This too is true.]

So Patsy was drawing on my insight and carrying it forward. "That's why lawyers rehearse witnesses so thoroughly, helping them tinker with their "eye-witness" testimony until it's air-tight. Mine did me. For the divorce."

"Yep."

"I read somewhere that we all lie an average of five times a day, and particularly to ourselves. We are really experts at self-deception."

"It keeps us happy, I think," I answered.

"Like you wrote. "Lying is the grease that keeps the world turning."

"Yup."

[Re-reading the last few paragraphs another zinger just beamed its way in. During the time I was painting for Paul, his fabulously wealthy mother-in-law was visiting, literally *dripping with jewels*. I had gone into the house to use the facilities and heard a vacuum cleaner running. When I passed Mumsy on the way back out she turned off the machine and said to me "This is amazing!" I nodded, though I didn't have a clue what she meant.

I later learned it was the *first time in her life* that she had availed herself of such a gizmo. As they say, "The rich are different." [Dollars to donuts she didn't breast-feed. She didn't strike me as a "do-it-yourselfer."]

But enough about my memories, what about Patsy? She's the protagonist here. [And was attractively curvy, I must note.]

She was thinking about her ex, a fellow she'd met in college

---

142 In the Foreword of *Self-Evident: We Hold These Tooths,* BUB, 2020.
 I'm always flattered when my characters read and reference my work.
143 Heiress to a massive frozen food fortune.

twenty-some years ago. They'd married after graduation and that lasted almost seven years. Fortunately, IMHO, they'd not made any babies, the presence of which always complicates splitsville. Like others among my characters there was infidelity involved in the break-up.

Sigh.

Rodger had always seemed wholly on—and above—board, and was as serious-minded as you might expect an electrical engineer to be—not that he *was* an electrical engineer, mind you. I just wanted to use a comparator that would convincingly convey the observable quality of his demeanor. He drove a jing-a-ling ice-cream truck in warm weather, cruising neighborhoods to tempt children into tooth decay, and operated a warehouse forklift in the cold months. (For the major frozen food corporation mentioned upslope, as it happens. Small fricking frosty world.)

Patsy was on her way to a paint job one day in June, 2012, and saw his ice-cream truck parked in a suburban drive.

"Hm," she thought. "Hmm." But being a trusting soul—recall that she was still in her 20s, a time when our brains have only just gotten more or less organized—she assured herself that he was probably delivering Eskimo Pies® for a birthday party, for "The Millers" as the sign on the house read, and continued to her place of employ.

Or ice cream bars? Or fudge-sickles?

That night when both arrived home she asked, "Do the Millers have a boy or a girl?"

"Who?"

"The Millers, with the birthday party."

"The Millers?"

"Where you delivered ice cream today."

"Oh, oh." He skipped a beat. "A daughter."

That would have been that but for this: a few days later Patsy passed by the same home and saw the rear bumper of the ice cream truck peeking out from behind the place. She braked and backed and parked her pickup and walked down the drive to be sure. Yep.

That night she confronted him.

"Millers have another birthday bash?"

"What?"

"Son or daughter?"

"What?"

"I saw your truck."

"Where?"

"There."
"There?"
"There."
"Where there?"
"Out back."
"Out back of where?"
"There.
"There?"
"There. Rodger are you double dipping?"
"Honey, you know all my cones are pre-wrapped."
"Not what I mean and you know it."
"No, I don't."
"Is Ms. Miller grinding your gear?"
"What?"
"Or is it *Mister?* I thought I knew you. I thought I could trust you. You've been cheating. How long? How long?" Patsy's volume knob was definitely cranked. With copious tears.
"No way."
"Way!" she shot back.
"How could you think ...?"
"How could you do this?"
"You're wrong ..."
"Well, of course I *could* be wrong. *Lots* of people order *lots* of ice cream. So we'll just drive over there and chat."
"I think you're taking this all too far."
"I'm going, whether or not you want to join me."

He didn't and she did. [I think we can infer that she *stormed* out.] By the time she arrived at "The Millers" she had regained her composure. She introduced herself to the young(er) woman who answered the door, who was *not* a Miller, rather a renter,[144] and like Patsy, child-free.

The facts of the matter were clear and Patsy ended with, "I hope you and Rodger are happy screwing. You sure screwed me."

To this Ms. Renter replied, "Who?"
"Your lover-boy."
"Who?"
"The ice cream man."
"Oh, you mean Ted."
"Ted?"
Patsy pulled a picture out of her purse. "Rodger."
"No, that's Ted."

---

144 We'll leave her name out of this. Too many monikers spoil the subplot.

"No, that's my soon-to-be-former. Rodger."

Ms. Renter was wide-eyed. "He lied to me."

"You and me both, hon. You and me both."

Lies may well be the grease that keeps the world turning as I once observed with my usual amusingly sardonic wit.

They are also slippery as hell.

Meanwhile, I've recalled my conversation with Patsy any number of times in the years since because she's used me as a job reference. Whenever someone contacts me regarding her painting skill ("No holidays!" I tell them, vehemently. "No holidays!") I think back to those days on my deck, balusters and all.

My clearest memory—and forgive me, but I'm a guy—is that she favored v-neck tee shirts which were pretty revealing. [So shoot me.] The rest of what I've told you is probably somewhat less accurate given how often I've remembered her "story."[145]

Then, too, she had often thought back about the events *she* described, being as they comprised a hinge-point in her life.

["Things we pull up frequently are changed each time we consider them." See first graf, page 63.]

Thanks, Patsy, for the ...

---

[145] Upper.

Events leading up to ...

How often do we hear that?

"Very" is the correct answer.

We're confidently informed that this or that particular "chain of events" resulted in "x." As if.

No, no, no.

Everything results in <u>everything.</u> It's like the Russian nesting dolls phenom discussed on page 48. The only reason there exists a smallest item when you start unpacking the figurines is that there is a practical physical limit when it comes to carving wood. So that example is symbolic, perhaps metaphorical, but granular? No. Ultimately—<u>meaning "in reality, i.e. *real reality*"</u>—the "dolls" would diminish in size until we reach the singularity—the eensy dot that existed the moment before the Big Bang.

Does this mean there is no free will?

Yes and no.

And isn't that interesting?

It certainly seems so to Evergreen Kelly.

E.G. ponders a lot. Thinking and then rethinking is his "thing"—a "thing" no one would ever have thought back when he was in school. Most of his cohort regarded him as thoughtless if they thought about it at all. [Personally, I don't think many did so-think.] But, obviously enough, thoughtlessness is a pretty blurry attribute.

"That was *thoughtless* of you!" [Jeez. I'm sorry.]

Then along comes The Buddha®, traipsing amidst bodies on the battlefield and encouraging his minions to seek "no-mind." The goal, obviously enough, being "thoughtlessness."

E.G. thinks about such things quite a bit while he's tinkering.

"With what?" [I hear you wondering.]

With clocks! Mechanical clocks! [Bet that was a shocker!]

Even in this digital age many people have a fond attachment to the timepieces of their youth, or those inherited. [If you are among them, E.G. is your man.] He understands the inner workings of all sorts of archaic chronometers, and can diagnose, disassemble, set the delicate works in order, then return the same, good as new. Alternatively, though with a heavy heart, if restorative surgery is impossible due to the ravages of time (odd how time's ravages can ravage a mechanical clepsydra)—largely preventable if some irresponsible owner had paid a bit more attention, just a wee bit—he will install an electric mechanism that will keep the gizmo moving *as if* all the old wheels were still at work. *As if.*

"It's a sad, sad shame," he'll offer, "but it was the only way to keep the mighty hands of time on track."

We're close, he and I, so sometimes I drop by his shop to chat whilst he's delving and plying. We banter about quantum physics and worm holes and probability theory. [The usual stuff two guys talk about when no one else is around.[146]] Oh, and special relativity. We're both pretty keen on that.

"Heisenberg was right," he'll observe.

Then I'll come back with, "And Thomas Kuhn."

He'll nod. "Right, Kuhn nailed it. And Gödel."

"Especially Gödel," I'll agree.

[After all, as Natalie Wolchover noted in *Quanta®*,[147] "Gödelian incompleteness afflicts not just math, but—in some ill-understood way—reality." Ultimately the obvious takeaway is that we can't conclusively prove anything at all.] [At all.]

E.G. will look away from the clock in current consideration, turning to me with pursed lips, then intone, "No one can fully fathom the meaning of incompleteness, y'know? I mean, you'll hear someone say that so-and-so is a 'complete idiot.' But that's impossible."

"Got that," I retort. "When the truth is he's actually an *incomplete* idiot. [Italics mine.] There's no other sort."

"Then there's that whole line of books '... for the compleat idiot.' and incomplete idiots actually buy them!"

"Crazy world out there, E.G. Crazy world."

What I like about these conversations is that I always leave feeling a little less certain, sort of like Heisenberg. As noted on page 39, humility is one of the most useful realizations in a human life. In fact, I didn't think about it twenty-nine pages ago, but that amounts to a general rule.

General Rule #7: "Humility is one of the most useful realizations in a human life." I'm pretty certain anyone over the age of, say, 45—when a brain finally gets its total groove—would have to agree.

---

146 Most guys won't admit this.
147 A magazine full of things that no one actually understands.

Just this week[148] the first photos from the James Webb Space Telescope® have been published. We can see further back in time than ever before, which also means further away, and the latest speculation—based on the new view—is that there may be a *trillion* galaxies out there. [Which means a lot—if your math awareness is a few bananas shy of a bunch.] Each with millions of stars. Which means there are something like a gazillion[149] planets.

If that doesn't suggest a little humility, what does?

Back when we thought the solar system revolved around us it was easy to think we were, or wore, the crown of creation.[150] But now, of course, we know better. We squat here on a smallish planet circling a middling star in an average cluster on the outer edge of a typical galaxy. If there aren't intelligent life forms out there who are *way* ahead of us in terms of drinkable boxed wine and sensible leisure wear I would be astonished.

But all this astonishment has sort of led us away from E.G. who is standing idly by, and who is presumably the subject of the current disquisition. [If not the "object."] [How, actually, do we disambiguate *that?*].

E.G. is kind of an "odd duck," though most of the guys who discuss the Fundamental theorem of arithmetic congruences[151] with him might not realize that. [His conversational interests are perfectly normal—see above.]

What he hasn't told pretty much anyone is this: he believes "free will" is a very convincing *illusion.* [I only know about this because I invented him.] If you were paying close attention you might have noticed that he nodded pretty enthusiastically when I offered that "*Everything* results in everything."

"That's it!" he thought. "The whole history of the universe has resulted in this particular clock spring that some incomplete idiot overwound. That reminds me of the Vonnegut® story in which the entire history of the earth, since Jesus® at least, has been guided by aliens[152] in order to facilitate manufacture of an

---

148 Writing this on 14 July, 2022.
149 An even larger number if you lost track.
150 Reminding me of the Jefferson Airplane® album of the same name on which the deepest, and maybe strangest, song is "Triad," written by David Crosby and first recorded on *Crosby, Stills, Nash & Young,* the album by Crosby®, Stills®, Nash® and Young®.
151 The other thing two guys are apt to chat about when no one else is listening in.
152 I don't recall if Vonnegut's® aliens were described as "mattress people."

item, later discarded by a human, which constituted a repair part that would be needed for the alien's disabled spacecraft centuries later.

"I didn't 'choose' to do this repair, or to go into this business any more than Vonnegut's® character had a choice regarding the throwing away of the future alien repair part. But ..." and here we insert a pregnant[153] pause ... "it sure *felt* like I decided. The sense of having free will is very convincing."

Very.

So there we have it, at least in the sense of feeling that we're in control, and, if everything, *I mean everything,* is determined by initial conditions, well, not so much.

Actually, not at all. Maybe only "free" in the sense of being given the illusion with no money down.

I thought you'd like to know.

Meanwhile this question from E.G. is a real stumper: "Where do thoughts come from? Hmm? You don't think them *before* you think them. So whence?"

SUBSEQUENT NOTE: In mid-October 2022 the Webb telescope detected oxygen and carbon dioxide in the atmosphere of an exoplanet, both considered to be tell-tale signs of biological activity. Stay tuned!

---

[153] Gotta wonder if pregnant pauses are affected by the 2022 SCOTUS ruling on Roe v. Wade. Can state legislatures now ban them like paused pregnancies? Will De Santis ban pregnant pauses in Florida?

Growth

A good thing, we mostly all agree, being as we want to be big when we're little, and want to know more or possess more once we're big, and are eager to have our three squares—which require growing plants if not animals—and so on and so forth, right up until we're informed that the MRI has detected one that may very well prove fatal.

Two sides to every coin.

Pat, at this point, is still keen on it.

He's done the up part and has the meal tickets covered, but he developed an expansive mood and hoped to fully grasp the "meaning of life."

A tall order indeed.

Where to hunt for it is clearly the first question, though, in point of fact, if there is an actual *raison d'être*,[154] it has to be everywhere at once. But it seemed at least possible, to Pat anyway, that there might be places where it shines through a little more, like the bald patch atop his head—which is to say, regions where the cosmic nubbin is less hirsute.

Of course he gave popular religious faiths a chance, being as they are "highly touted" and tried really hard to see the glimmer. However the three or four majors and several minors all came up short. Many hats and no cattle, so to speak. All taste and no nutrition—like spiritual diet soda.

Then he tried navel-gazing. Lint was not the answer.

I think that amounts to General Rule #8: "Lint is not the answer."

Video games seemed plausible, given the amount of computing power devoted to the genre, so he gave them a shot. Nada. Nothing in the medieval, the nearly unimaginable future, the "build it and they will come," the super-heroic, the erotic or the kids' collection shook him to the core.

"Maybe," he thought, "the answer is dietary." So he binge dieted, figuring that three months at a "go" would be long enough to get some sort of result. Veganism, fruititarianism, soyism, ovo-lactoism and then a swing to pescatarianism and the paleolithic, even liquid—nothing lit his lightbulb or jingled his inner doorbell.

---

154 Been a while since we enjoyed us some *française!*

"Hello?"

You with a proclivity for higher math have already figured that the food adventure took a year and three quarters. (!) And if we apply his three month rule to Judaism, Christianity, Muslimism, Jainism, Buddhism, Shintoism, Hinduism ... and a handful of others—plus the gaming—we extend his search several more years. [He didn't go a full term on the navel business, by the way. Recall General Rule #8. He's smarter than that.]

The Church of the Flying Spaghetti Monster® got him a good bit closer to closure, what with the midget pirates, and he went with Pastafarianism for half a year, practically feeling the "noodley presence." But that kind of blurred the line with the diet plans. The idea of eating the godhead seemed a little too much like the blood and body parts implicit in Christian communion.[155]

Then Pat read "It's the little things," (p.53) and a light bulb appeared above his head.

(I just doodled this while doing my morning crossword.[156])

"Math!" he exclaimed. "Math!" [Pause.] *"It all adds up!"*[157]

Per navels.[158]

---

155 Reminding us of George Harrison®'s "My sweet lord." Tasty, eh?
156 Executed on 11 August, 2022. The puzzle itself from the NYT® archives, Friday, 11 February, 2005.
157 Emphasis his.
158 While navel gazing and lint still adhere to General Rule #8, navel gazing per se can be of immense worth. Yesterday, gazing at my navel (an "innie" as it happens), I discovered a tick. (!) "Ticking away the moments that make up a dull day ..." is one thing. Being ticked away is quite another.

If at first ...

... you don't ... blah, blah, blah.

Maybe, sometimes, but the flip side is maybe you're aiming for the wrong target. All those months and years of "trying" may well be a waste of precious time. It's not like you're going to be around all that long. None of us are.

Madeleine got with the program early on and she's started more projects than you can possibly imagine only to quit at the first hiccup. Her measure of success, you see, is how many things she's *attempted!*[159]

No "one-trick-pony" she.

She studied *Español*[160] for a full afternoon, she applied for a job as an airplane mechanic,[161] tried out for the local symphony,[162] thought about building a cell tower,[163] wrote the first two lines of an epic poem,[164] considered planting a tree,[165] decided to take up photography,[166] and filled out *most* of a formal application for an educational grant—all of that just last week!

Breathtaking isn't the half of it!

I could go on, but in short order we'd all be out of breath.

So perhaps we'd be better off considering Madeleine's sister, Jennifer.[167]

Jenny is in love, and that is just so darn nice I bet you have a smile on your face already, even without knowing who or what this woman loves. Love is pleasant, and as we have discussed more than once in these pages, pleasantness is not only pleasant but, as we read in footnote #111, it has been touted by Annie Dillard® as the best response to a grizzly bear. [Once again I'll politely suggest "You go first." ("If at first ..." could be a problem in this scenario.)]

---

159 Including, astonishingly, robbery!
160 *Español!*
161 Sans experience.
162 Sans instrument.
163 For at least ten minutes.
164 But got stuck on a rhyme for "orange."
165 But couldn't settle on a type.
166 Didn't.
167 I feel better already.

So. Animal, vegetable or mineral?

Well, unless you're a veritable Scrooge McDuck® a passion for mineral matter seems kind of "out there." This suggests that we not saddle Jen[168] 'with, say, a profound fondness for, oh, I don't know, maybe molybdenum.[169] Or graphite.[170]

So, lets flip a coin. [I am actually going to do this. Heads: animal. Tails: veggie.[171]]

Hmm. No loose change hereabouts, so I'll flip a debit card. [Same rules apply.] ...

Vegetable it is.

Your author has now painted his sweet self into a corner. And also, very likely, dampened your enthusiasm regarding Jay.[172]

"In love with a vegetable? Really?" [I hear you thinking.]

Well, in her defense I have to point out that remarkably few vegetables talk trash about ex-lovers and they only rarely cheat,[173] they are good listeners, they pretty much never interrupt, they are generally available 24/7, most don't smell funny, they don't intrude, they never use your toothbrush or your razor, they don't hog the covers, they don't fart, they don't use your credit card to buy some kind of stupid thing at the mall, they don't forget to put their dishes in the dishwasher, they never go on and on with stories you really don't need to hear, and they "grow on you" (assuming you have some space). [Growing on you being a characteristic of items in the first graf on page 71.]

Duly noted:They don't have at it with the landlord whether the "having at"is for better (licit) or worse (illicit).

Also, and not to be diminished, they don't vote, meaning they don't vote <u>against</u> you, cancelling yours) whatever angle you might inhabit. I mean, really. Really?

"Are you suggesting ...?"

I am.

---

168 Notice that we *have* saddled Jennifer with two hypocoristics in just three grafs.
169 I know this will draw harsh reviews from all of you molybdenum worshippers out there, but I can live with that.
170 Ditto.
171 It's unclear to me whether this constitutes a hypocoristic.
172 Yet another. Only Jennifer's close friends call her this. "Hey Jay!"
173 The squash family being a major exception here, interbreeding like the denizens of Tippy Toe Lane, explicated in the totally gripping tale "Knotted and Tangled" in the astonishing collection, *Waist Not, Want Knot.* BUB, 2020.

Irked

Haven't we all been? At one time or another? Except maybe those totally, entirely, annoyingly chill people who meditate a whole bunch and manage to go un-irked for years at a go? Decades? Lifetimes? (See page 79.)

[But, dunno. Maybe they're faking it?[174]]

Not most of us (I think it's safe to surmise.)

But, still. Couldn't we at least consider Chelsea?

Well, of course, being as we are nice people. We will.

Chelsea, consider yourself considered.

Eloise on the other hand. Y'know? Eloise is wracked with guilt over something she did "years and years ago" (months anyway, "wracked" denizens being somewhat prone to hyperbole) —which, try as she might, she just can't get past. It was in a physics class where she asked, "Why is the probability given by the square of the amplitude?"

You could have heard a pin drop. Or a black hole implode.[175]

'Self-locating uncertainty"—the professor finally broke the silence—"Self-locating uncertainty. I'd like to see you in my office after class."

Fat chance that. She'd heard what supposedly happened to young women who "saw him in his office after class" and wasn't going near that with a ten foot pole *and* a taser *and* a bucket of ice water. So she never got an answer and it has troubled her ever since.

But why the guilt trip?

I thought it more than obvious, but, whatever. She realized later, *after* she dropped out of the class—and, subsequently, college—that she had interjected a question that she just *knew* left her classmates in an utter quandary. They were already stumbling through the "many worlds" approach to quantum theory and she had posed a question that would haunt them **forever.**

How many other young women had, therefrom, following in her disparate academic footsteps, voiced the same query and

---

[174] "Prior to this lifetime, I surely was a tailor ..." Paul Simon®, "Fakin' it," *Bookends*®, 1968.

[175] This is what qualifies as a physics joke. Sound waves don't travel in a vacuum. But more on black holes on page 88!

made the mistake of "seeing him in his office?"[176]

All of which was ultimately her fault. Was it not?

She shuddered to imagine what then transpired. Professor Ramses Montalbaño would have towered over the innocent girl, clearly presenting a moral, if not mortal, threat—fight or flight? <u>Fight Or Flight?</u>—and would then intone: "There are unique answers to quantum Sleeping Beauty problems, my dear."

"My dear?" Really? "My dear?"

Can you actually imagine a more triggerish trigger phrase? Do you think he'd dare say "My dear" to a male student? ["No" is the correct answer.] He'd say "My man," or "My young sir," or "Mr. so-and-so."

Eloise <u>knew</u> she would have been seriously irked. Really, really, really irked. Beyond that, she had led others, Bo Peeping the flock so-to-speak, to experience that same diminution that she, herself had—albeit, brilliantly—successfully avoided. She'd (however inadvertently) therefore, and sadly, left her then-cohort of female physics students wide open to irkedness.

It's no wonder she has trouble sleeping.

Montalbaño, of course, had/has no clue regarding his irksomeness. He was simply old-school and referring to young women as "my dear" was entirely intended as a kindness. He loved and loves theoretical physics. He loved and loves inquisitive students. His invitations to his office were an up-looking effort to offer one-on-one guidance to inquiring minds. There's not a prurient bone in his body.

Well ... maybe that last is a little too squeaky-clean.

Better said: There are no more prurient bones in his body than in the rest of us, but those pruriencities are not directed toward (or expressed relating to) his students. He's what we might say is "off campus kinky."

"Leather and Lace"[177] as Stevie Nicks® framed it. Montalbaño would agree. ["I am stronger than you know."]

But we won't go there since this story is about someone else entirely. Eloise. Remember Eloise?

Eloise, or "Elly" as her friends know her, lives in the distal branch of the universe where she dropped out of college as versus the universe where she plowed on through a doctorate and eventually won a Nobel® in theoretical physics. One of the nubbins that bugs her noggin is the question of whether that

---

176 Sans ten foot pole, taser and bucket.
177 On the album *Bella Donna,* Modern•Atco®, 1981.

other branch still exists, [or maybe "ever existed"] given that she bailed. [baled?][178] Or are there infinite branches?

The idea of "many worlds" is approximately opposite that of the "everything results in everything" rubric previously discussed in this volume. The "E~E" equation suggests that everything is inevitable: ie. "No free will." (Even if it feels free: e.g. "I feel free," *Fresh Cream,* Cream® 1966.)

MW on the other hand suggests infinite free will. Each decision creates a new iteration of the multiverse, everything splintering from the get-go. The tough nut then becomes, "Can any of the others be observed from here?"

"What if?" Elly wonders in the wee hours—"What if she'd stayed in school and switched to a psych major?" Or, who knows? Art? Biology? Chemistry? Math? Cartography? Ooo. Oooh. Cartography! Cartography!

Were there other Ellys who did those things? Does Many Worlds mean Many Ellys? Or does it mean that the entire universe she inhabits abruptly hit a nodal point when she left Montalbaño's classroom? Furthermore, doesn't that mean that every decision at every moment creates a new one?

This certainly casts the wonderful joke on page 49 in a new light, does it not?

Further furthermore, doesn't that suggest that when I make a decision it must bifurcate <u>your</u> universe as well. Are you with me so far?

[Whew! I was afraid I'd lost you when I decided to get dressed and head out to un-coop the chickens.]

[Time passes.]

[Back now. Chickens out and fed.] So the question then becomes, "Did the universe(s) branch when I *decided* or when I <u>actually got dressed</u>?" If I had lain here writing, naked as is my wont in the predawn hours, and decided—but not actually <u>gotten up</u>—would anything have bifurcated?

I think we are dealing with a Martin Luther® thingy here.

Of course Marty framed it as the question of salvation by faith or by acts and, if I remember correctly, an argument against selling indulgences. Faith, it seems to me, involves a decision—in this instance a choice to believe in an imaginary deity.

Are there imaginary deities in all of the Many Worlds? Or just a few? If not in all, there are many of us who'd like to learn of

---

178 See page 54 per "bated" and "baited." Same puzzle, different consonant.

the decision point that would gain entry to one <u>without,</u> given the endless mischief created by believers in same. A world sans "believers" sounds pretty darn heavenly to many of us.

But I digress.

Whilst tossing about in the wee hours Elly has been wracked[179] with the certainty that a degree in cartography would have helped her map her life. Maybe make a Venn diagram to figure where everything fit? A nautical chart to tell her where best to set sail? Or, for that matter, to drop anchor?

She's lately been talking that over with Chelsea.[180]

Chels is considerate—one reason we considered her in the first place—and therefore is a good listener, well prepared with good questions. "How does that make you feel?" "Where do you want to be in five years?" "Do you want to walk to work, or take lunch?"[181]

Then the nubbin-rubber. "Why don't you go back to school?"

"Oh, Chels. At my age?"

"Are you thinking 22 is too old or too young?"

"Both."

Chelsea frowned. "If that isn't self-locating uncertainty, I don't know what is."

"I know Chels. I know. It irks the hell out of me."

---

179 This the third use of this word in this gripping tale and I thought to, perhaps, find a synonym. Scouting around online I was reminded that "wrack" is dried seaweed, which is certainly something to think about.
180 See? Mentioning Chels up top was intentional, not some random act of kindness.
181 This still cracks me up.

Swim-Swam-Swum

Okay. I'll confess. The title of this story [which occurred to me in a weak moment] will very likely have nothing to do with the wildly amusing narrative that assuredly ensues. But isn't it fun to say?

Go ahead. Say it several times . (Note: Faster is harder.)

I'll wait.

[I bet more than a few Transcendental Meditation® patrons have been handed that one as their "secret" mantra.] [Funny, I haven't thought about TM® for many, many years, but it just now occurs to me that those paying customers could all have been given the same "secret" mantra and none would be the wiser.[182] Heh, heh. S-S-S.]

[Nor am I typing that S-S-S lightly, being a certified Red Cross® lifeguard—which is factually true—but of no particular relevance to the following story.]

Dorothy (Dotty to her friends, and Dot to her bestie) is a crabber. (We didn't see *that* coming, now did we?) (Whooie!)

There are, we note, other alliterative things she might have been, but isn't, at least not principally: Grabber, nabber, stabber, blabber, dabber, slabber and jabber come quickly to mind.

But no, Dotty actually *traps crabs!* [We here immediately realize that I am a friend but not her bestie. Gloria is her bestie.]

Being a crab trapper one supposes makes her a grabber and nabber, but only collaterally. She has traplines laid out in the Gulf of Mexico from her home port of Cedar Key, Florida.

My A-list readers (both) will recall that Dotty isn't the first Cedar Key crabber[183] to appear in my vast catalogue, but trust me, she is different in significant ways.

First off, kind of obviously, gender, though I *could* be pulling a "Boy Named Sue" trick here. But no. Then, too, she's not the town drunk. Then, three, she obeys the fisheries laws—no short claws off the stone crabs and definitely never taking both.

---

182 Except, of course, those apostates who "told." But, believers being believers, one must assume there were few. Is TM® still a "thing?"

183 Pete who we met in "Tern, Tern, Tern," in *Fifty Wheys to Love Your Liver,* BUB, 2018—the crabber who took Angela of "Angie's Lists," out on the Gulf. Surely you remember?

Pete was a poacher. There are few apples badder.

For the 99.785 percent of you who somehow missed that story I should probably explain that with stone crabs an honest crabber grabs and nabs just one claw off a two-clawed victim then returns the little critter to the deep blue sea wherein the crustacean normally re-grows the missing limb. If, like Pete, you routinely snapped off both limbs—or the remaining one off the victim of a previous crabber-grabber-nabber (CGN)—the shellfish soon dies of starvation, having no way to convey food to its mouth. Adding injury to insult, so to speak.

You'd think enlightened self-interest would make that sort of thing go "without saying," since you want the harvest to continue into the future, but Pete wasn't the sharpest hook in the tackle box, and also, as we've seen, a scofflaw. That he ultimately fell overboard and drowned while drunkenly trying to paint Angela's name on his stern, upside down one must surmise—if you can picture it—leaning over the transom, brush in hand, wobbly as the dickens, when a swell rocked the boat fore and aft. Splash.

Well, crab *food*, at least. "Instant karma gonna get you ..."[184]

When Angela returned to Cedar Key some years after her first visit she asked another fisherman she'd met back then how Pete was doing. Tommy told her, "Couldn't have been long after you were here. Went out, drunk as a skunk, might've been that morning you left here. It was a few days later one of the guys found the boat. A lot of talk. There was an open can of paint. Looked like he must have been leaning over the stern, renaming her. Letters were pretty shaky, painting upside down with the boat rocking. Looked like he must've fell out while he was doing it. No paintbrush. Just the can of paint. A-N-G-E-L and the beginning of another letter. Lot of superstition here abouts. Some said he knew he was going to die, naming his boat Angel."

"Oh," Tommy added. "Oh. Another letter."

Well, that got her to thinking. "Oh," pause, "oh!"

I see a hand up. I know you're imagining this is what the story title referred to, given that it reflects the presumed final trajectory of the former CGN. Actually, no. I didn't intend to mention Pete at all, but as we have learned, there's no telling where thoughts come from.[185] He just wandered in here, so to speak. Or boated. (Sailed?) And drowned.

---

184 John Lennon®, Plastic Ono Band®, "gonna knock you off your feet."
185 See page 60.

But that story has been told and we wanted to get to know Dotty, who, by the way, had "interacted" with Pete, though he was about twenty years her senior. The crabbing community on that little island is not extensive. Then too, when he was jacked up he hit on every single-woman in town and most of the married ones as well—cautiously excepting those whose husbands convincingly brandished firearms.

Pete, as you likely surmised, had grown up on Cedar Key and never left through three marriages and as many divorces. Dotty on the other hand had gone off to college, earned a degree in marine biology, and been hired by the Florida Fish & Wildlife Service®. As a side-gig she'd started crabbing (and grabbing and nabbing). After a few years of enforcing the rules she realized that she loved the ocean more than the badge and quit her "day job."

Like Pete she savored the freedom of being her own boss, motoring out of the mist-shrouded harbor at daybreak toting a bucket full of mullet (for bait, not lunch), with gulls laughing overhead, pelicans doing their aerobatics—all in a line, undulating with the swells—the terns skimming for breakfast, and dolphins rising and blowing ahead of her little craft as the mainland disappeared from view. Plus, the solitude. That was the deal-sealer.

She pulled her traps and thought big thoughts, never worrying where those thoughts came from. Kind of idyllic when you think about it. Also, she had a nice tan (sometimes working in the "altogether."[186])

On the day in question (yesterday, actually, which is why she was able to tell me last night so's I could write it down this morning) Dotty was thinking about coffee filters. Talk about deep! (Which, we recall, is what Pete is asleep in, metaphorically.)

She buys hers, the unbleached sort, in stacks of 200. I think we're all familiar with such, are we not? Her puzzlement—which accompanied her through miles asea and pulling many yards of rope from buoys to traps, hand over hand, and the C-ingG-ingN-ingS-ing[187] and the baiting[188] and tossing and etcetera and so forth —was this. How are the damn things stacked so precisely? Y'know, with the little pleats all the way around? She observed, "They can hardly be stacked up one at a time, right? So what? I mean, how? Huh?"

---

186 Giving some readers one of my arguably famous hot'n'steamies.
187 See footnote 188.
188 For which she had to cut up the mullet, making her a stabber as well.

Consequently she'd tried to imagine how the process might go with some sort of circular blade and some kind of piston shoving the filter papers into some kind of tube, maybe? And it can't be one stack at a time, can it? So are there hundreds of circular blades with as many pistons, ditto tubes, all with plastic bags beneath? And then the twist-ties. Is that a manual thing?

I guess you can see what I mean about Dotty. She's super inquisitive. Heck, I would never have thought twice about those stacks if she hadn't brought it up.

Today she has a new thinky thing to be thoughtful about. But we'll have to wait for tomorrow. I'll call her tonight to find out.

(The previous was written on 9 October, 2022. Now it is the 10th.)

Well, well. Yesterday Dotty was thinking about something else entirely, which is how thinky people go pretty often. Another day, another thought.[189] After she talked with me two nights ago, at the bar, when I bought her a beer, she was on the phone with Gloria. Y'know, her "bestie?"[190]

Gloria, my goodness, is up on the Olympic peninsula just now, in Washington state, in the Olympic National Park! (!) That's about as far from Cedar Key as you can get in the contiguous U.S.

And here's the thing: in addition to marveling at the enormous trees, the astonishing slugs, and the fearless wildlife, Gloria has seen a nest. "A" nest? No, three!

"Dot," she said. "I saw three nests!"

Of course a lot of the "trees" on the peninsula are stumps these days—stumps that measure 12 feet across—and the banana slugs at almost 10 inches are slimily interesting, but the nests? The nests are nearly 10 feet in diameter! Big Bird®?

Come on. Big Bird® is either a non-gendered puppet character on Sesame Street® who clearly doesn't need a nest, or an emu or ostrich neither of which species reside in North America—other than on farms.

What some folks believe is that these huge nests are created by sasquatches. [This is a real "thought thing," not of my

---

189 In this case coming from Gloria, so at least we know where this thought came from.

190 See page 79.

invention.]

As of this writing serious scientists are doing DNA analysis of material in the nests.

No, really.

"Dot," intoned Gloria, "Dot there are real scientists doing DNA tests on material from the nests. This isn't something this Bothwell character came up with. How do you know him anyway?"

"He was here on vacay and he bought me a beer."

"Oh, hitting on you like Pete?"

"Nah, just being friendly near as I can tell. But he did ask about Pete. Seems he'd gone out pulling traps with him back in the 70s."[191]

"Bothwell must be old as dirt."

"Yeah, but he seems OK."

"Anyway, Dot, you know gorillas make nests, right?"

"But not here ..."

"Right. In Africa. But why wouldn't a sort of proto-human build a nest here?"

So you can see why Dorothy thought about that all day yesterday. Three nests. Three!

Sasquatch! (?)

Deep!

---

191 True. And I did go back to Cedar Key some years later, though I wasn't actually there this week, and I did really learn from another fisherman about Pete's S-S-S, which is why he landed in my stories about Angela, though that isn't his real name. "Shoes for the dead, shoes for industry!" as Firesign Theater® framed it, on *Don't Crush That Dwarf, Hand Me the Pliers,* Columbia Records®, 1970. [I just now listened to *Don't Crush,* on 12 October, 2022 to confirm that recollection. It is always satisfying to discover that one's memories are affirmed. Though, of course, if we are actually living in a Matrix®, that would still be the apparent "lived experience" and the memory.]

Oh, wow!

Nathan. Pity poor Nathan. A moniker forever linked—in American commercial pop culture—to hotdogs.

What *were* his parents thinking?

I mean, if the family name had been, say, Hale, well OK. "Only one life to give for my country" Enobling! Or, heck, I don't know, Brosnan or Herald or Wilson ... not so bad ...

But Weiner? I'm sorry, but that just doesn't float. Pasting a kid with that combo amounts to cruel and unusual.

It's no wonder he calls himself Nat[192] (rhymes with gnat not *frate*[193]). There's not much to be done with the family name, of course. Maybe "Way-ner?" Certainly not "Whiner."

Be that as it may.

Here's the thing, though, Gnat has a girlfriend!

That should be enough on its own, but it gets better! (!)

She owns a lunch stand!

She sells hot dogs!

Irony, or what?

It's a little trailer doohicky that she parks down by the courthouse weekdays. Jurors and judges and plaintiffs and defendants cluster about, biting wieners or chicken tenders. Hennie[194] rakes it in!

See the reason for the "wow!"? (Up top, if you missed it.)

None of that is particularly interesting, of course. Still, Hennie is fascinating in her own right. Oh, indeed! (See again, "Oh" up top. "Oh!") Else I would not have dragged her in here.[195]

Hennie has a dragon tattoo! (As versus a "dragged in" one.)

But that's not what makes her interesting (except to Gnat when they get gnaked). (I mean, you can't see it when she's clothed.)

Gno indeed.

---

192 The same Nat we met on page 71. I can't be expected to invent new people all the time. I mean, I do have a life!

193 Meanwhile a "frate"is a friar in Italy, as versus a fryer, perhaps in Hennie's deep fat. One needs a score card to keep track.

194 See? This story isn't about Gnat.

195 Nor was she kicking and screaming, though that might have made this a more evocative tale.

Hennie gnits! While waiting for customers. And she gnits serious messages like a regular Madame Defarge!

She works out her angst in gnitty gnots.

Given that I've now compared her to Ms. Defarge you might infer that Hennie is an *angry woman,* shouting things like "Then tell Wind and Fire where to stop, but don't tell me."[196] But you'd be way off base.

She's more worried than angry, though sometimes she's a *little angry* that she's so angsty. But why is she angsty just now, a few weeks before the annual Christmas parade?

Well, she is to be re-borne. Or, rather, borne again.[197]

You see, she is also a member of a local *théâtre*[198] group. You know—the kind of outfit that does the *Santaland Diaries®*[199] every year at a community playhouse?

Well, they also participate in the yearly exercise intended to encourage excessive consumer spending by revving up the "holiday" spirit. Buy more! Buy more! Buy more! Tra-la-la-la.

But the thing is, she has long, straight, black hair. Naturally black. And a kind of Egyptian complexion and nose. [She might be Jewish, but she doesn't say.] Doomed, obviously. (To a role she never sought.) (A *théâtre* "role rule" is to accept any role you are qualified for and voted into by the other members. Or face expulsion from the troupe. Harsh? Eh, what?)

For several years the Mountain Théâtre Collective® has centered their Xmas contribution around Hatshepsut®, the first woman pharoah.

So their—kind of retro, if you ask me—entree, features "Hatshepsut" (with Hennie as the Hatshepsut-ee, hair, nose, etc.) on a Nile-themed float. [What this has to do with Christmas is a mystery I'm not prepared to explore.]

The Pharoah Hatshepsut (or "Queen"—but the Egyptians were generally gender-neutral in their designation of rank) often wore a beard, sort of signifying that while she was a woman she ruled as a man. (So yes, Hennie wears a beard.) Whatever. But this doesn't exactly bear on the present story.

Gno.

---

196 Dickens® if you skipped high school English.
197 Which might have been a better title for this story.
198 Yes! *Française!* They sort of "put on airs" while also putting Hennie "in the air."
199 The David Sedaris® idiocy, which, at least in the performance I saw here in Asheville several years ago, was tasteless and disgusting.

The thing is that on the aforementioned float "Hatsepshsut" is held aloft in a sedan[200] chair by six stout sedan-chair holders!

So there we see Hennie/Hattie in a gold- and silk-bedecked conveyance, on a gaudy parade float, with rampant asps (figurines, not live snakes) and an image representing the sun-god (Ra, Ra, Ra!), held aloft by six muscular men, stripped to their waists (in order to evidence their bulging muscularity and their immunity to the cold) and oiled and swaying with the rolling of the road and undulation of the muscular support of the massively muscular men ...

But we've seen this show before, three years ago in the last Xmas blowout, right? Pre-pandemic.

Hennie/Hattie was being conveyed along the parade route and one muscular sedan carrier stumbled. What with the oil none of their grips was particularly good. The sedan-chair fell.

!

Hennie was unhurt but suffered permanent reputational damage. "Oh,[201] *that* woman who messed up the Christmas parade? Yeah, *what a loser*. I hear she sells hot dogs and is hooked up with a guy named Nathan Weiner. Har, har!"

She's been living that down ever since. So the prospect of being re-borne is angst-making. (Though, to be clear, the jurors and judges and plaintiffs and defendants still cluster about to munch lunch.)

What she's considering now is going to a shrink and getting a Xanax® scrip. Her bestie Susan told her that it really helped with her panic attacks. But Hennie looked it up online. Yikes!

MISUSE OF XANAX® CAN CAUSE ADDICTION, OVERDOSE, OR DEATH.

Susan, Hennie has discovered, is hooked. Oh[202] boy.

So now the tangle is between fear of being borne and fright regarding a potential back monkey. Nobody needs a back monkey. [See Lynyrd Skynyrd® reference on page 93.]

Hence the knitted x-es and o-s. (X for Xanax® and O for "Oh!"[203] when she worries about Susan.) (The current project is beginning to look like a complicated tic-tac-toe game.)

Susan, we here note, had no intention of getting too deep

---

200 More about sedans in the following story.
201 Another "Oh."
202 Yet another.
203 Again. (And three "Oh"s on page 80. Strange, or what?)

into drug dependence, but panic is a harsh mistress. In the beginning she was panicked into immobility regarding dinner prep. She was so fearful that she'd burn the rice or spoil the salad that she couldn't even *start*. She'd sit at the kitchen table and try to convince herself to measure out a cup of basmati, but ... but ... but couldn't bring herself to stand and walk to the cupboard.

"I'll just burn it."[204]

She'd know there was romaine and arugula in the fridge, but she just *knew* she'd pour on too much balsamic vinegar and wreck the greens.

"They'll be inedible."[205]

Well, the Xanax® changed all that, thank goodness. Now she's a cooking fool![206]

But. Always a but.

Now she gets panicked when she thinks about kicking the Xanax®. "What if I can't cook without it? Will I starve?"[207]

You see?

Meanwhile, back in the mobile deli, the pattern emerging is X-O-X-O ... As if, perhaps, Hennie is gnitting a love letter?

Kisses and hugs gnittily gnotted in Egyptian cotton yarn.

How sweet.

---

204 Anxiety can be a force for good, actually. It could have motivated her to become a better cook.
205 Ditto.
206 But her results are, sadly, approximately inedible and she often resorts to microwave-type frozen dinners.
207 See footnote #206.

Mystery Solved

One of life's little'uns. But every such step marks progress toward the day when <u>All Will Be Revealed.</u> (!) Socks in the laundry, y'know?

Penelope has figured it out. Credit where due. Credit where due!

Why do they so frequently *not* emerge in even numbers? Your author has been so troubled by the phenom that he has for many decades purchased only white and black[208] versions, and to the extent possible—despite the vagaries of modern manufacture—identical ones. The sock drawer is a sort of singles bar where a lately divorced piece of footwear hangs out, relaxed and optimistic, waiting to meet someone new.

That obviously solves the problem, but not the mystery.

To be clear when I was young and scrambling I used a laundromat and the absence of mates could be attributed to the greed of the commercial operator whose machines were designed to pluck socks out of a load for sale on the second-hand market. But in latter days the laundry never leaves my house.

Into the washer. Slosh, slosh. Spin, spin. Into the hamper. Out to the line. Hang, hang. Four pair in, seven socks out.

Oh, I *have searched*.

And it is madly random. Everything hunky-dory[209] for months at a time. Then, whoosh!

Now you'll just have to take my word that mine is a relatively modern gizmo Yes, with a filter.

Lint, of course. The occasional nickel. Socks no.

Penny though, is a thinker and a reader, two qualities which

---

208 White for summer, black for winter, mix it up in spring and fall.
209 Reminding me of David Bowie's® fourth studio release of that name with it's opening song, "Changes," and it's haunting truism: "Time may change me, but I can't change time." Oh, and "Turn and face the strange." (Advice I have ever since taken to heart.) RCA Records®, 1971. (Note: Bowie did not hyphenate his record title. But he was a Brit and hyphens may have been in short supply what with the Conservative Party reserving them for aristocrats. Parker-Bowles, Mountbatten-Windsor, Rice-Davies and so forth.)

very much endear her to me. Last week she was doing what so many of us seem to do so much of the time: staring at a screen.

[Side note: Do you recall what we did with ourselves a decade or so ago, say in the waiting room at a doctor's office? Back then you'd find a diversity of magazines to which the doc subscribed to give you something to do between glancing at your watch. The subscriptions were a prescription for patients to instill patience.] [How a practice could be running late at 8 a.m. was and is another mystery. I'll maybe ask Penny to look into it.]

Where was I? Oh, Penny. Screen.

She stumbled on an article on the phys.org® website posted in May of 2011. "Mini black holes that look like atoms could pass through Earth daily."

Whoa! Don't black holes suck up everything in arms' reach? Like cosmic Shop-Vacs®? Like Hoovers® run amok? Aren't they extremely massive? Mini? Really? Are they going to run us over?[210]

Well, doing some intensive research over the course of nearly 15 minutes Penny learned that these minis are so tiny they *almost never* run into us or anything else. They were apparently formed in the Big Bang® immediately after the Singularity® blew up into every thing and everyone that presently exists.

Big black holes[211]—the scary ones—form when a star collapses on stage. Too many shows in a row, too many drugs and drinks, too much limelight, too much adoration, and so forth. Bang!

Anyway, Penny has come to believe that every once in a while one of these mini-things hits a sock during a wash cycle, when the garment is wet, confused by the spinning, and helpless.

I know. That sounds pretty crazy. But most of quantum physics is worse. Meanwhile, if we slice this with Occam's razor ("Entities should not be multiplied beyond necessity.") we see that Penny's answer is simple and elegant—elements that are highly prized in theoretical physics—whereas my allegations about the owner of a laundromat are complicated and silly.

Have you ever bought second hand socks? I thought not. "Turn and face the strange," indeed.

---

210 Another website she visited said that these little boogers are as massive as 1,000 sedans! (See footnote 200.)
211 Correction: I heard a radio show on the topic 29 November 2022, weeks after writing this. Massive black holes are actually quite tiny because of the intense gravity. Also they are more location than "thing."

Suite Dreams

Like Joni, y'know. Checked into the Cactus Tree Motel® and dreaming of 747s® over geometric farms.[212] There are some things we only dream about when we're away from home.

Remember Terry who we met way back on page 13? Yesterday he was telling me how his dreams when he sleeps in the fire tower are much different from those he dreams when he slumbers with Carol,[213] though calling the box on stilts a "suite" is probably a stretch.

He has nightmares when he sleeps alone on the pine boards, worrying about the coming (or current?) alien mattress invasion. With Carol he sets aside his worries and enjoys very pleasant phantasmagorias.[214] La-la land in the best sense.

[Oh, they are getting on *famously!*[215]]

Quentin has had the same experience, though he sleeps neither on the floor (at home), nor with Carol, though the latter idea has crossed his mind. He's a regular Ranger Rick® and works out of the same office as the object of Terry's affection. He's just a little jealous as well, but, hey, he could have asked her for a date way back when. They *are* friends, which is nice.

Early birds get the worms, you know.[216]

Quentin's territory is large so some nights find him hours away from home. Rather than make a long nighttime commute only to get up early and drive back, he rolls out a sleeping bag (on the floor) in a shelter-half or cabin or tent deep in the woods, eats some trail-mix and reads by flashlight. The kind of upstanding/down-lying guy we all admire.

Oh, does that take me back. Zap. A memory I haven't

---

212 "Amelia" on *Hejira,* A&M, 1976
213 Yes, they've gotten much better acquainted during the past eighty-some pages. I bet your glasses are getting pretty steamy, eh? These explicit scenes really get most readers going.
214 Though we here note that when she's in another room of her apartment he occasionally punches the mattress to see if there are any signs of life.
215 Two steamies on one page! This is getting to be a regular *Valley of the Dolls*®-type episode!
216 Though this always makes one wonder about the early worms.

revisited in decades. [And talk about hot'n'steamy!]

I went on a three week bus adventure with a group of Boy Scouts®, from Florida to Colorado in 1965. It was a well-planned jaunt and probably cost my parents a ton. We stopped at various historic sites along the way including the Alamo® and saw a major league baseball game, I think in Houston. We arrived at the wilderness camp drop-off at night in a rain storm and had to hike-in a considerable distance with our personal gear. [There were wall-type tents waiting on platforms in the campsite.]

My young brother[217] slipped and fell in the mud and was on the verge of tears, so being the kind of guy I am, I hefted his pack as well as mine for the balance of the trek. For many years thereafter he deemed me to be kind of his hero, which obviously felt pretty good. But that's not where this story is headed.

On our return to Florida we spent two nights in cabins at a Scout® camp before our parents picked us up. It was hot and fairly miserable, particularly when compared to the Colorado mountains. There were no screens, or perhaps inadequate ones, and to ward off mosquitoes one had to stay completely inside a sleeping bag. That's the hot part.

The steamy came along just before Taps®. Somewhere, this part I don't recall, I found several magazines that were not G-rated. It was my first exposure to fairly lurid descriptive material. Whether it would qualify as porn today, I don't know, but it sure got my attention. By flashlight. Inside the sleeping bag.

Hot'n'steamy!

Quentin's reading material is far more high-minded.[218]

But before we get back to Quentin, around whom this story revolves, the previous true story has now reminded me of another episode, or series of episodes, that occurred perhaps two years later. So I would have been about 17.

We lived on a lake and had a boat moored next to the dock I had helped Dad construct a few years previously. Most of our neighbors did the same, generally hiring out the dock-building part. The doctors who lived two and three doors down had pretty elaborate boats with cabins, whereas ours was a simple runabout-type ski boat.

We children of privilege often hung out on the boats, particularly the cruisers which subbed as our clubhouses. One day I was alone on one of the fancy ones, waiting for the son of one of

---

217 RIP. He reached his date of expiry in 2012.
218 Like many of my characters he owns several of my titles.

the docs to show up, and being curious, if not nosy, I lifted a triangular cushion in the bow. OMG! A thick stack of Playboy® magazines! I quickly replaced the lid, my youthful heart going pitter-pat.

As you surely imagine, I didn't tell a soul, even the friend who shortly arrived. We joked around about whatever 17-year-olds joked about in 1967. Did he know? Were they his dad's? His?

But as you can also surely imagine, being a Boy Scout® I adhered to the motto, "Be Prepared!" Armed with a penlight that night—and many thereafter—I raided the stash taking and returning one at a time, turning the erstwhile clubhouse into a lending library. Fond memories of youth. Sweet dreams indeed.

But back to the tale at hand.

Quentin told me about a difficult experience he had while sleeping in a lean-to shelter adjacent to the Appalachian Trail®.

It was a moonless night and the stars were in their glory.[219]

He had been asleep a few hours and woke from a fairly terrifying dream involving some sort of beast, more in the form of a nameless threat than a recognizable form. Being an experienced woodsman, regular animals don't much frighten our protagonist, but this threat was way outside the norm.[220] His teeth were even chattering a bit.[221]

That's when the bear walked in. [You see, there is no front on a lean-to shelter. Always open for business.]

Obviously enough, Quentin, being who he is, had no food in the building. He didn't even have any food in a sack on a rope slung over a branch. He'd eaten his trail-mix before he left his U.S. Forest Service® pickup at the trailhead.

But here's the thing. Waking from a truly terrifying dream on what we previously learned was a moonless night, he could hear the snuffing but he couldn't see the animal. He recognized the sound alright, but a black bear doesn't exactly stand out in a dark place with no ambient illumination.

Well, starlight, yes. As mentioned upslope stars were in their glory. Twinkling like mad. Like there was no tomorrow. But

---

219 For you wannabe writers out there, setting a scene this way is to practically guarantee consideration for a National Book Award.®
220 A mattress? See the first story in this collection if you've forgotten.
221 Although he didn't mention this, he almost certainly had an erection. I've recently read a study which found that most healthy men do when waking from a dream. Hence the phrase "morning wood." Thought you'd like to know.

would there be a tomorrow for Quentin?

Now he could smell the beast, kind of a wild odor ... not skunky, maybe more foxy. But definitely gamey. The kind of smell that you might have smelt if you ever petted a wet Labrador retriever. Or, maybe if a raccoon set up camp under your house. Musky. Not altogether unattractive, which is the reason why musk oil is used in many perfumes.

We often get a whiff when we pass a dead skunk on the highway. It can be overwhelming, or, with sufficient diffusion, kind of nice.

The barely visible beast sort of snuffed over his way then padded to the other end of the small structure. It made kind of an oomph sound and settled.

Quentin was taking very cautious breaths at this point. Black bears are not generally aggressive unless they are protecting youngsters. So presently, in our (his) narrative, he figured things would be OK.

That's when the two cubs stumbled in. He could tell they were youngsters by the pacing of their paddy-paws and their higher pitched snuffing. They seemed to go to the adult bear and he could hear some kind of grunted greetings. Then what sounded like licking. He waited. Things got quiet with the grownup, presumably a Mom, even snoring. Quentin was gathering himself to make a quick and quiet departure when one of the cubs ambled over to his side and settled against him with one forearm over his leg.

Well, needless to say ... but why should I follow that idiom by saying it? I mean, if it's needless. Right?

Of course we know our guy survived, else he'd not have told me that story.

My guess was that he didn't sleep well, and I was right! He told me he was petrified, afraid to move! But, in the end, he dozed off. It had been a long day and a harsh night. Also, cuddling with a teddy bear can trigger childhood memories.

When he woke, with a start—and likely with an erection: see footnote #220—the bears were gone. He even thought for a moment that all of it had been part of the nightmare.

But then, there was that smell. [Reminding Quentin and all of us of Lynyrd Skynyrd's® lyrical treatment of back monkeys.]
"Oo-oo that smell
Can't you smell that smell?[222]

---

222 *Street Survivors,* MCA®, 1977

Short Sharp Shock

We were going to get back to Celine and as we close in on the halfway point in this collection it seems as good a time as any. All we really learned about her was that she was in bed, naked,[223] with Carol's theretofore main squeeze (and Carol's sister) and that she owned two dogs. Not much to go on there.

So, let's see. Having two dogs she probably doesn't have a job that requires a lot of travel—like say, flight attendant or long-distance trucker. She might rent but it would be better if she owned her own place with a fenced yard. A single woman owning her own place at a relatively young age must have a pretty remunerative gig (or a substantial bequest).

I've got it! She's a <u>veterinarian!</u> She calls her practice "Don't Worry, Bark Happy!®" (Which I admit sounds pretty silly, but the smiley dog on her logo makes customers smile. I'll drive over and take a picture. Hang tight ...)

That didn't take too long did it? Thanks for your patience! Isn't she a cutie? Name of Buttons and yes, she's one of Celine's pups. Don't you just want to take your pets there? Maybe Buttons will greet you at the door and you can cuddle!

If you don't have a pet (what?) maybe you could just stop by anyway. If they question your motive say you're thinking of getting a Pom and the sign pulled you in. Then ask, "By the way, does Buttons have any puppies?" That's sure to endear you to Celine and her staff.

[No. Spayed.]

But back to Celine herself. So, we know her profession and her business name. Let's see, um, her other dog is a rescue. A retired greyhound! Named Stretch. She's a bottle-blond (Celine, not Stretch). [Don't get me started.] And frisky.[224] [Ditto.]

But here's the thing you wouldn't have guessed about this woman: she plays dead. No, really.

---

223 Doesn't that just give you the flutters?
224 As illustrated on page 23.

This is a *real* hobby that *real* people *really* engage in. [Though not very many.]

She would stage her own death in front of a cell phone on a tripod set to "video," then clip out the best parts as still-shots and post them on Instagram®.

I've seen her head-down in a plate of food, sprawled at the foot of some stairs, splayed in the back yard with Stretch sniffing at her "lifeless" form, collapsed over the steering wheel of her car, and the "plain vanilla" variety—lying in bed with her noggin on a pillow, tongue hanging out, mostly covered in a white sheet. The naked one—where she's fallen out of the shower, torso twisted so as not to be overly revealing—got a lot of "likes." [Nudity is ever thus.]

This isn't what most of us have come to expect from our veterinarians, now is it? [Type "Celine-veterinary-dead-naked" in DuckDuck to see that one. Whooie!] [Whooie!]

There's kind of a competition among dead-players who aim to create the most convincing scenes.

A couple of years ago some fraudsters muddied the field by posting pictures of people who had actually just died. No sense of good sportsmanship there, but—of course—it helped honest players refine their game. As Pablo Picasso® (and several others) said, "Great artists steal."

"Why?" I hear you asking. [Regarding the playing, not the stealing which is self-evident.]

Well, that's a puzzle. What are these dead-players hoping to achieve? I suppose bragging rights. "Nyah, nyah, nyah, nyah, nyah. I look deader than you do!" Though, obviously, we'll all look convincingly dead sooner or later, and that's not something you can actually practice for, no matter what George Harrison said. Rather, sang.[225]

But, of course, Harrison pulled it off back in '01—practice or no. Arty or artless.

So Celine was constantly thinking of new scenes where she could appear expired. On the pavement behind a bus. Twenty feet below a cliff. Drowned. On railroad tracks—though the severing of limbs requires a pretty handy hand with Photoshop®. [Hand presumably still attached.] In a crowded mall? [Malls, we recall, in this continuing time of cholera—and the ascent of Amazon®— were once crowded.]

---

[225] "Art of Dying," on *All Things Must Pass,* Apple®, 1970 "Then nothing sister Mary can do, Will keep me here with you."

But then Celine upped her game!

There's this other group of odd hobbyists who engage in "extreme ironing." Yes, that's a *real* thing. Hoo-boy.

What they do is tote an ironing board to an extreme place, say atop a mesa, or deep in the jungle, or on a glacier, or on a surfboard, or in the cone of a volcano, and ... get this ... iron a shirt. (!)

But Celine (bless her heart) decided to go them one better. (!) [Gotta love this woman.]

Celine's new thing was to copycat extreme ironers but then die across the ironing board. (!) It's like garnering Gold Medals in two Olympic® events at once! Here she's collapsed over a steam iron on Mount Washington, there in a heap while pressing a shirtsleeve in Key West.

I think we were all thus inspired. Go Celine, go!

Me? Me, I wish she'd been turned just a little to the left in the shower shot. But I may not be a good person.

Oh. The shock mentioned in the title? Well, in her last set-up Celine bit into a steam iron cord to lend verisimilitude. What she didn't know is that 110 volt power is potentially fatal. The jolt clamped her jaws shut. That final photo was real and very, very, very convincing. She was, as they say, flattened.

Meanwhile Buttons and Stretch are available for adoption.

Art Imitating Life Imitating Art Department

About a month after writing this story I was listening to my favorite news program (*Wait, Wait Don't Tell Me,* on NPR®) I learned that police in London lately responded to an emergency call regarding a person, viewed through a window, head down and motionless in a bowl of soup (or possibly cereal). The bobbies broke down the door and rushed in to find a "dead" mannequin—part of an art installation. This proves something—and not an iron in sight!

Upper crust

To get the obvious out of the way from the get-go, the upper crust is always the flakiest. [Take that as you will, you upper crusters!]

Reginald Armbruster is no exception. Though silver-spooned at birth, spoiled from the outset and privately schooled, he didn't make the *most* of his cushy start. I guess if one never has to really *work* for anything there's no need to tuck in one's shirt, pull up one's trousers, zip one's fly, pull down one's hat brim, tie one's shoes, look in the mirror and face the music.

The trouble with being a flaky playboy is that most people figure you out pretty quickly and then don't much want to play.

[This reminds me, for no apparent reason, of Mason Williams'® prince who was eaten by his panties.[226]]

Reggie is flaky in several ways. I'm sure you can imagine.

His few friends simply shake their heads and say to themselves, "That Reggie." To the extent that he has any *amigos* at all it is largely due to the fact that he generally picks up the tab, which says as much about them as him, or so I infer.

Are you for sale? I thought not.

Nor am I.

Anyway, yes, he's a flat earther for one thing, though at the same time be believes the globe is hollow and inhabited by aliens. He also believes in Ikea®. If he was a reader [and he is not, even declining the proofing of this story] and had perused the first tale herein he would likely start talking to mattresses.

I suppose that means that Terry (pg. 13, et. al.) might be considered "flaky" as well, and—given his work situation—"upper" applies, if not "crust" but there is a fundamental difference between believing something one reads and *theorizing*.

Terry theorizes.

---

[226] The prince had 100 cocker spaniels. The only thing he loved about them was their panting, hence he called them "panties." To make them pant he "ran them ragged," and their reaction was to consume him. *The Mason Williams Phonograph Record,* Warner Bros., 1968. On the first printing of the record the track title was misspelled as "Princess Panties," making that version more valuable to collectors.

In any event, non-readers are *ipso facto*[227] flakes.[228] IMHO.

[Did you notice how I slipped in a Latin phrase? Classy, eh?]

Also, and this may be the worst ... Reggie *doesn't listen*.

But that's not what this story is about. It involves dinner(s) at a fairly posh restaurant. Redge, as some of us call him, invited five friends to dine at La Bamba®—on him, as usual—to celebrate the introduction of purple M&Ms®, a candy brand of which he is inordinately fond.

La Bamba® had been hiring of late, which was helpful to Mitch Evans and Larry Trout who had recently been relieved of their duty on the local police force due to budget cuts. The age old labor policy of last-in/first-out had, sadly, been applied, although when they were recruited to the La Bamba® waitstaff they were pleasantly surprised by the pay increase.

Evans and Trout had trained under Detective Jason Newsome and Officer Bill Pronke, the duo made famous for their good cop/bad cop interrogations.[229] They got more beans spilled than any other team on the force and the trainees brought their acquired skillset to the new job. (Though with a somewhat different approach to the spilling of beans.)

On the night in question the servers chatted at the start of their shift.

Trout: "I want to be the first bad waiter tonight. I'm in the mood.

Evans: "Fine with me!. I'll go second"

When Redge and company had been seated and given priceless menus (i.e. no price listings, high end or what?) by the *maître du restaurant*[230] the new waiters stepped to tableside.

"Good evening, I'm Mitchell and this is Lawrence."

The other added, "We'll be your servers this evening." He then added, "Could you get out of my way?" He gave one of the diners a bit of a shove. "I think I left my gum here." He reached under the table, felt around, and then appeared to put something in his mouth.

---

227 Latin!

228 I can get away with this kind of broad-brush characterization because I know that if you've gotten to page 98, you are not one of the above. Also, I bet you're excited! Only two more pages until we start the downhill run!

229 See footnote 97.

230 You can tell it's a classy joint when this is written *en français!*

Mitch proceeded to take drink orders while Larry chewed.

"Not mine," with which he again nudged and returned the "gum" to its place of origin, then headed toward the kitchen.

"Nice choice," or "Excellent," or "My favorite," was the waiter's response to each beverage choice except the last which was to stick with water. "Of course." After taking the orders to the bar, Mitch quickly returned with a pitcher and filled the crystal water goblets all around while the guests continued their animated conversation.

"That gum trick!"
"Couldn't be real."
"But if if was?"
"Hilarious!"
"Gross."
Etc.

*Then back to the usual uplifting discussions of upper-crusters everywhere—divorces, stock splits, homes in the Hamptons, private jets, yachts, Beemers[231] and Rolexes®.

Before long Larry returned with the drinks on a tray. As he set a tumbler of Johnny Walker® in front of the first diner he commented, "Sticking with the cheap stuff, huh? That say's a lot about a man." He made similarly disparaging remarks regarding two house-gin martinis, and a house-brand Manhattan, but reserved a more cutting remark for Jeremy Bonners who had ordered Sangria. "Can't drink with the grownups, can we?"

Finally he addressed Norm Clayton. "Water, huh? Guess you're fighting that drinking problem." As he stepped away he knocked Clayton's spoon to the floor, picked it up and set it back beside the man's plate before departing.

"I never!"
"Who does he think he is?"
"What a jerk."
"The rudeness!"
Etc.

Fifteen minutes passed as the conversation settled into the usual. (*See the 8th paragraph upslope.)

Mitch returned.. "Have you good gentlemen made decisions regarding appetizers? I particularly recommend the Citrus-Pickled Oysters on Toast. It's our chef's specialty."

Again as he took orders his comments were upbeat. "Ah the oysters, good choice. Ah, the bacon and date, can't go wrong

---

231 No ® because this is not a registered trademark.

there. Another oyster, you'll be glad you chose that." On and on around the table. Finally Clayton ordered the Crab Rangoon and the waiter said, "Ah sir, you clearly have refined taste. Excellent decision! Oh, a clean spoon? Certainly." He returned quickly with the replacement, then, off to the kitchen.[232]

"Polar opposite."

"Can't wait to taste the oysters."

"Top notch!"

Etc.

(*See the previously referenced paragraph.)

Meanwhile, in an adjoining dining area, Larry stepped up to an 8-top. "Good evening. I'm Lawrence and this is my partner Mitchell."

Mitch added. "We'll be your serving team this evening." Then he gave a nearby diner a nudge, reached for his "gum" under the table top and popped "it" in his mouth.

Larry continued, "I see we're celebrating a birthday this evening! Congratulations Ms. Ratner! Mitch and I will make sure it is a happy one! To start off I'll be pleased to take your drink orders." He went around the table, jotting notes on an iPad®. "Good choice! Ah, Sam Adams®, that's patriotic! A Gibson, of course!" And so forth.

"Not mine," Mitch offered, gave the patron another nudge and stuck the "gum" back beneath the table.

"I never!" was the only response from the nudgee, one Paul Landry. After both waiters left there was some amused chatter before the conversation returned to the usual banter of used car salespersons everywhere.

"I absolutely scalped a woman on a 2016 Tacoma®! She paid at least $500 over book."

"That's pretty good, but I took a guy for a major ride this morning. Almost $1K over book on a Beemer."

"My way is to low-ball the trade-ins instead of bumping the sticker. Then I clean up on the next sale."

Etc. (We'll designate this convo with ** instead of *.)

Soon enough Mitch showed up with the beverages. "I see we're all sticking with the cheap stuff tonight. Well, it's your livers, not mine." He proceeded to set tumblers and high balls around the table. As he reached to deliver the last of these to Landry he said, "Oh, a Manhattan! Love me a Manhattan!" He

---

232 Note that we have reached the midpoint. Only 100 pages to go and you'll be out of this morass. All downhill from here!

took a long gulp from the stemware before setting it down and heading back toward the kitchen.

"Do you believe that?"

"I'd ask for a replacement if I were you."

[When Larry returned—see the eighth graf downslope—he handled the request with aplomb.]

A bit later Larry returned to Reggie's table with a large tray which he set on the adjacent stand.

"Let's see, you wanted the oyster mess, right? Do you know what those things eat? Disgusting." Next came "Bacon? Seriously? Breakfast food at dinner time? Where did you grow up?" Then "I warned your buddy over there about the oysters." And so forth until he served Clayton. "Ordering Burmese in a Latino themed restaurant seems like a really, really stupid move. Maybe you need a drink." He walked away, guffawing.

"What hole did he crawl out of?"

"Can you believe?"

"No tip for that one. I feel sorry for his partner."

Etc.

(*See the previously referenced paragraph.)

Leaving that table Larry rounded the corner, assured Landry that a fresh drink would be promptly provided and requested *hors d'oeuvres*[233] orders. "I would point out that the Crab Rangoon is one of our chef's specialties." With orders accepted he headed kitchen-ward.

Snickering and car talk (**) ensued.

In a few minutes Mitch appeared with the replacement drink. "Not much for sharing, are we?" He swapped out cocktail glasses and took another long gulp from the first, shook his head and left, returning to Reggie's table.

"How is everything? I'm sure you're enjoying things. More drinks? And are you ready to order entrees?"

Soon he had lists of both and headed to the bar and kitchen.

Larry returned with the second round and collected empties. "Oh," he said to Clayton. "I saw your dinner order. Really? Really? Fellow, you definitely need a drink. Maybe a jello shot? I see you ordered the *machaca*. At least you're off of the Burmese crap, but have you ever seen that stuff? Looks like vomit to me." He snickered as he left.

"I think we need to speak to management."

---

233 It's clear that the French *appellation* is more impressive than the prosaic "appetizer."

"Maybe bring it up with his partner?"

"No tip for that jerk. I bet Mitchell loses out."

Etc.

(*See the previously referenced paragraph.)

Mitch came back to "see how everyone is doing."

Ted Armour spoke up. "Mitchell, your teammate is unbelievably rude. How do you put up with him?"

"And disgusting," added Ben Willis. "Really disgusting."

"Ah, I wasn't aware. I don't know him that well, but I thought him a hard worker. I'll have a word with him, and please, please accept my apology for whatever he's done. Now, your entrees will be out in just a bit, but is there anything you need right now?"

Redge ordered two bottles of *Faustino®*, a Spanish red.

"Scotch, neat. Make it a double." Clayton paused. "Glen Morangie®[234]."

"Certainly, sir," then with a little bow he added, "The best of the single malts!"

In short order Mitch returned with the drink, the wine bottles and six crystal *copas de vino*. He uncorked one bottle and handed the stopper to Redge who squeezed it approvingly, then poured a dash into the host's goblet. Redge tasted and nodded and the waiter, noting patrons' affirmations, poured wine into four of the *copas*. "Enjoy!" Then off to the kitchen.

"Night and day."

"A credit to his upbringing."

"Or training."

"Every waiter should be so good."

(*See the previously referenced paragraph.)

Next Mitch picked up the birthday appetizers and delivered them to the salespeople. "So, you all fell for that Rangoon pitch? Our chef never made that crap before tonight. Hadda bunch of fake crab meat, you know, made from some kinda junk fish? Going bad. Hadda do something with it." He strode off shaking his head.

Larry arrived with the Reggie meals. "Bunch of damn tattle-tales, huh? Can't stand a little honest criticism, huh? Look, you high and mighties. I need this job and you're trying to get me fired?" He slammed down plates. *Chilorio* scattered, onions flew from atop pork *enchiladas*, a splash of *pozole verde* splatted into Armour's lap, a chunk of *carne asada* fell into Willis' martini, and

---

234 Does Scots count as a new language?

a piece of *pollo mole* landed on the floor. The waiter snatched it up and returned it to Reggie's plate. "Ten second rule." Finally he delivered Clayton's *machaca*.[235] "Off the wagon so soon? You'll need it. See, it *does* look like vomit." He spilled the side dish of refried beans on the table, picked up the tray, stomped off, then gracefully approached Ratner's group.

"How are we doing? I see you haven't touched your *hors d'oeuvres!*" Informed of Mitch's disparagement he replied, "Oh, Mitch. What a sense of humor. Nothing wrong with the crabmeat at all. And I assure you it is *real* crab. I ate a couple myself when I came on duty. Delish!"

One and then another of the auto merchants gingerly nibbled, then dove in. "Now, are you ready to order entrees?" They did, along with more drinks, and chit chat returned to the biz. (**)

At the first table Reggie was laughing. "What a character!" He cut off a piece of chicken and forked it toward his mouth.

"Redge! You're not going to eat that!"

"Ten second rule," and he popped it in, chewed, then down the chute. [He evidently listened in this case.]

Armour wiped a few drops of soup off his trousers then sampled a spoonful. "Mmm. Quite tasty."

Willis fished the beef out of his drink, tasted it, and proceeded to dip more of the *asada* in the martini. "Really good," he affirmed.

Clayton was pushing his *machaca* around on the plate, but not eating, clearly uncomfortable with Larry's characterization of the meal. Finally he waved to get Mitch's attention. "I need another double," he implored.

"Certainly my good man. It's my favorite too."

Following a big gulp of his second drink Clayton tasted a small bite of the shredded beef. "Actually pretty good, no matter what that asshat had to say about it." He proceeded toward what my folks always called the Clean Plate Club®.

(Conversation soon settled into what we heard in the *previously referenced paragraph.)

Mitch delivered the next round for the birthday celebrants. "Sticking with the rot-gut, are we?" Then to Landry, "I see you ordered the *machaca.*" He sighed. "Don't say I didn't warn you, but that crap looks like vomit to me."[236]

---

235 Note how many words in this paragraph are *en Español!*
236 We see here how these teammates have shared ideas.

I don't think we need to further belabor this as I'm sure you can imagine dessert orders and so forth based on what has transpired so far, including *flan* in a wine glass and a chunk of *pastel de tres leches* on a shirt front, Mitch knocking over a wine bottle at the Ratner table and Larry loudly farting at the other.

When Mitch delivered the check to Reggie the host placed his plastic card on the tray and pressed cash into the waiter's palm. "This is for *you,* sir. Please don't share it with your rude partner."

"Whatever you say, good fellow. Whatever you say."

The bill was crisp and Mitch knew from his police work that the crisp ones hadn't much circulated, meaning it was almost certainly a Big Ben. As he slipped the money into his pocket he found he felt at least two notes. (!) He smiled.

Back in the kitchen the waiters split the 200 bucks and Mitch told Larry, "Worked as usual. That's like a 30 percent tip! Good job, bro. Good job!"

The tip at Ratner's table was less generous, used car folks being notorious tightwads.[237] But 15 percent is 15 percent and it was a big tab. I don't think Mitch was any less bad, nor Larry less good, but they are still learning the ropes. Their future's so bright ... dark glasses fer sure.

---

237 True fact, and you know how fond I am of such. My brother (RIP) did a stint as a used car agent and sold me a vehicle, assuring me that he'd gotten me the best possible deal and that he'd even declined his commission in the process to save me money. I learned from one of his co-workers somewhat later ... he had not. Also, it was a serious lemon. That was in the mid-90s and I soon traded it in at a *different dealership* for an excellent truck I still own.

Möbius B.

Why his parents named him that is probably beyond the scope of our purview, so we'll just have to hope that he's less "one dimensional" than he appears at first glance. Unlike poor Nathan (page 84) the name is *not* an embarassment, and perhaps even intriguing. More often than you might guess a new acquaintance has asked, "Get around much?"

Frequently, when he was looking for work, he was asked that during a job interview. "Funny," he'd rejoin, "how often that comes up. I suppose so."

Meanwhile please note: His fairly high-minded and scientifically oriented parents did not carry the mundane (if not somewhat suggestive) surname "Strip.[238]" They are of French extraction, or at least Dad is, and bear the moniker *Boucle*.[239]

So who is this man, more or less redolent of Flatland®?[240]

Good question. I could have asked it myself.

But I am averse to diversion and digression as you have come to appreciate. There are more important reasons to consider *M. Boucle* than who or when or why.

I don't suppose you noticed mention of *M* in the recent investigation regarding airbags, but it matters more than you might expect. A man imbued with a mysterious function of geometric flatness involved in the recall of thousands of units intended for globular unflatness? That is exceeding strange. [Of course the recall involved airbags that *didn't* inflate, so I guess the "flat" part bears some relevance.]

But why did *Pouf*[241] *Incorporé*® decide to employ a Flatlander as lead engineer on it's airbag design team?

As ever it's not what you know but who, or to whom you are related. *Père Boucle,* that is to say *René Boucle,* was a co-founder of *Pouf*® and though he's long since stepped down from his top

---

238 Those of you thirsting for hot'n'steamy can run with this. Just think!
239 "Loop" *en français*.
240 *Flatland: A Romance of Many Dimensions,* Edwin A. Abbott, Seeley & Co., 1884. If you haven't read it, I don't think any explanation here will be sufficient.
241 "Poof" *en français!*

management position he still owns a lot of stock. A lot!

Also, *M* had worked for *Pouf*® in summers during his college years—in a warehouse,—so he was coming around again.

At the time the company was faced with a hiring decision *M* was looking for work. The current managerial team decided that a bit of nepotism was no prob. What they managed to overlook was that *M's* field of expertise was in the design and engineering of wastewater systems. An engineer? Yes. An electronics engineer? No. [Airbags are essentially digital devices coupled with balloons.]

Oops. [*Pouf!*[242]]

Why they didn't stick with the original fully functional model is attributable to the unshakeable urge of corporate marketeers and managers everywhere to come up with new and improved anything.

Just this week I purchased a brand of corn chips I have fairly frequently consumed for years. The design on the bag was slightly different I guess, not that you'd likely notice—but for the announcement on the upper corner: "New Look!"

Why people would buy corn chips based on the appearance of a bag is an ineffable mystery. To my way of thinking the blue chips illustrated in the middle of the bag's beige front told me all I needed to know: blue corn chips. Same chip depiction as in the "Old Look!" version, near as I could tell.

Now—of course—if market research indicated that a redesign held *more appeal* to a test group of chip nibblers, I'd hardly argue that a new design held no purpose. But if that were the case would we need to be told that it was a "New Look!"?

And even if the chips themselves were redesigned, as long as the taste was the same would anyone complain? ["Y'know dear, I really liked the triangular ones better than the trapezoidal."]

I note that the bags of the other brand of chips that I also occasionally purchase are blue rather than beige, also with an illustration of the items therein, so one operates on the assumption that the chips inside the bag are also composed of blue corn.

However, the fact of the matter is that I like both brands equally well and my choice is based entirely on the current price per ounce, "New Look!" or no. [Actually, had they spared the artistic effort (meaning money, obviously) and passed along the savings in the form of an incremental price reduction, they would have further encouraged my brand loyalty.]

---

242 No ® here because we are using it as an interjection not a trademark.

Looks have even less meaning in regard to airbags since most of us will never see one and if we do we are more likely to be happy that we're alive than to be weighing consumer choices. At age 72 I hadn't seen one until last week when a young friend totaled his car. I was called in to recover a pricey radio that he was unable to extract and there were the two blue[243] airbags, fully inflated.

"Well, well," I said. [I would have been every bit as excited if they'd both been printed with "New Look!" or, more likely, "Surprise!"]

In any event after *René* left *Pouf*® management the new CEO waited a few years to make his big move and leave his indelible thumb print on the outfit. He hired a new marketing firm[244] which polled people who had seen airbags up close and personal. None of them reported being exactly happy with the experience (outside of being alive, obviously). They made comments like, "That's the last thing I wanted to see." Or, "Scared the hell out of me." And, "Horrible, just horrible." The marketeers concluded that customer satisfaction could be improved with a more appealing design and so came up with a new color scheme.

That idea was turned over to Möbius and crew who decided if the appearance were to be improved then the function ought to be spruced up a bit as well. In the course of more than a year they reimagined airbag design from the dashboard out.

I have to guess that the purchasing departments of several automobile manufacturers are populated by the kind of people who buy corn chips based on the "New Look!"

Pouf Plus® "New & Improved Look!" units were soon installed in tens of thousands of vehicles. Then it was only a matter of time before a great many accident particpants *didn't* see airbags when they should have.

The class action suit is going to drive *Pouf*® into bankruptcy. Layoffs have already begun.

Pouf![245]

M is back to Point A.

[Looking for work.]

---

243 Hence encouraging my use of the blue corn chips example.
244 The same one that redesigned the chip bags. Small world!
245 Interjection.

Title

In the middle of the night I awoke from a lurid dream[246] and had a brilliant idea for a name for the following tale, but failed to write it down. This morning it hath fled. So consider that **bolded** word upstairs a placeholder. Maybe it will come back to me as I wander around downslope.

The principal fly in that ointment is that this was to be a story about something that *didn't* happen. There may be few extant clues. It's even hard to know where to start. Before? After? Perhaps *while* it wasn't going on? A conundrum.

One possible launch pad could be looking up that idiomatic phrase. Where *did* the fly come from? It turns out to be from Ecclesiastes or Ἐκκλησιαστής for you Greek speakers, which is a translation from the Hebrew קֹהֶלֶת. (The Greeks obviously had extra letters lying around.) But the accepted English translation of the Latin transliteration of the Greek translation of the Hebrew phrase is: "Dead flies cause the ointment of the apothecary to send forth a stinking savour." [Love me some bible talk.]

Sorry I asked. That one's going to chase me around all day. "Stinking savour"? Eew! I'll try to pretend it didn't happen which gives me an opening. If I concentrate my attention and focus my thinking then that web search will constitute something that didn't happen. However, being in the moment, I clearly can't tell you what happened *afterward* since afterward hasn't happened yet, so I'll have to pick up the thread back when.

Let's see. You already know I woke up with a light bulb over my head and managed to forget the magnificent thought after falling asleep and waking again at 3:30 a.m. (I'm an early bird which is where I catch all these wiggly wormy yarns.)

OK. It was the day after Thanksgiving (just two days ago as I clamber around in this word jungle). Cleveland and I both avoid shopping on that day, given the madhouses that constitute Black Friday emporia. (Something that "didn't happen," at least for him and me.) [I've heard that things are less wild and wooly now that most retailers have begun offering the purported "deals" a couple of weeks early but I still demur. This too shall pass.]

---

246 See footnote 220.

This suggests a digression that I think bears mentioning.

(This is one <u>true</u> part of the current adventure.)

A friend of mine wants to purchase a washer/dryer—one of those all-in-one stacked things frequently seen in apartments. That's the reason she wants one. To see it in her apartment.

I priced identical units at two retailers, one a building supply and the other an electronics/appliance store, (online shopping for local pickup). Both websites offered the w/d for $1299 at a savings of $95 under the "list" price. A couple of weeks went by and I checked again. Now the first outfit promised me savings of $250, while the second stuck with $95, but both priced the unit at—you guessed it!—$1299. Finally, on Thanksgiving, I got an e-mail from the first vendor promising blow-out savings on Black Friday. Now I could save $350 if I forked over the low, low price! $1299.

Does that actually work? Are consumers that dim? [Not that saving $350 as promised in the subject line didn't *sound* good. My heart went pitter pat ... but that sale didn't happen either.]

Now back to the untrue parts.

Cleveland and I go way back. We used to work together at an orange juice plant in Orlando. It was an after school job when we were juniors in 1967. What we did was load pallets of orange juice in cartons in boxes onto refrigerated semi trailers. We got to horse around with the fork lift and we were allowed to drink all the OJ we cared to consume, beginning my lifelong addiction to the stuff.

Anita Bryant®, who later became a right wingnut (rightwing nut?), used to tell the camera that "a day without orange juice is like a day without sunshine." Sorry. I call BS. A day without OJ is like a day without heroin. Except that I drink it rather than smoking or injecting.

All of the OJ info above is true except my inclusion of Cleveland. That part didn't happen. We didn't meet until the spring of 2014, but he's a nice fellow and I thought he'd appreciate participating in my adolescent memories.

So, 2014. We met on a plane headed for Egypt! We just happened to be seat mates and quickly hit it off. Luck of the draw.

That was a pretty fantastic two week jaunt. Pyramids and iconic sculptures and camels. Camels! The buzz of crowds bustling amid street stands and the quietude of evenings on the banks of the Nile. I can still picture the fishing boats coming back from a day's work with fishermen hauling their catch ashore and handing the slippery silvery sardines—or whatever they were—to the women waiting on the beach. The women were in charge of drying and storage and I can still recall the smell of dead fish dehydrating in the blistering North African sun. (viz: stinking savour, flies and all.)

Oh, and later the venture on the Marrakesh Express. Wild ride, that one!

Only, of course, there is no such train, or at least no train with that specific name. The Moroccan town is Marrakech. Also, full disclosure, Cleve *did* go to Egypt and Morroco in 2014, but I did not. Didn't happen.

[He told me about it later and his descriptions were so vivid that it *felt* like I'd been there with him.]

I did meet him that year however. We were both called for jury duty and got to know each other while we waited for jury selection to proceed. We pretty quickly discovered our common interest in breeding Siamese fighting fish which is a pretty abstruse hobby. I'd guess that most of you reading this have never even *thought* about doing that. So you can see how this would have drawn us together.

Betas don't get along which is why the modifier "fighting" is included in the longer name. They have gloriously ornamental fins and if you put two males in the same tank they will quickly shred each other's ornaments, often leading to a mutual debility if not death. Even females get abused in such a situation which leads one to imagine that in whatever version the fish first existed, before the onset of hobbyist breeding, the girls didn't much hang with the boys. (i.e. another didn't happen)

But if you put a boy beta and a girl beta in the same aquarium with a glass panel between them he shows off, flashing his colors and the girl gets hot and bothered, soon swelling with eggs. Meanwhile the boy decides to impress her by blowing bubbles. (I'm not making this up.) The saliva—(I think that's what it's called)—coated bubbles adhere and soon he is the proud owner of what is called a "bubble nest," a little island of white froth.

Next the glass divider is removed and a chase begins. She shows off her round little tummy and he makes a dash, then returns to the nest and fans his fabulous fins, clearly inviting her to hook up. Finally she agrees and when she submits he wraps himself around her and squeezes eggs out as he squirts milt.[247] He then swoops down and catches the eggs in his mouth and spits

---

247 I bet you didn't see this hot'n'steamy coming!

them in among the bubbles, over and over until she's empty.

Now you have to remove the mom because she's exhausted and hungry and would like nothing better than some eggs for breakfast. Meanwhile, basking in the afterglow of conquest, the guy will devote himself to hatching and then child care. (I don't know if betas are closely related to seahorses, but the dads in both species are very nurturing.)

Oh, neither of us was actually tapped for jury *duty* and while I *did* breed betas many years ago (1970-71) I have no idea whether Cleve has a clue regarding fighting fish. The topic only sprang to mind 10 minutes ago. (Two "didn't happens" in a row!) But, of course, he *might* have. I'll ask if I run into him again.

What I do know about Cleve is that he was a terrific baseball player in his youth. He made the minors, which takes a good bit of talent and hard work. No, he never made it to the big league, but he led his team to multiple pennants. He was a regular 5-tool player frequently knocking balls out of the park, stealing bases, plus catching and throwing with the best of them. He played any position including taking the hill. Why he never got a call-up is a puzzle, but it didn't happen.

After five seasons he tired of the travel, the locker rooms in second rate facilities (stinking savour and all), the dashed hope, the strained muscles and the low pay. He simply quit. Now he sells insurance I think.

But I still can't remember that great title.

<u>Three days later:</u>

On the advice of an appliance repairman we trust, my friend decided to reject the washer/dryer unit and opt for full size, stackable units of a brand deemed "best stackable" in consumer reviews. I found an actual discount (I think they are unloading overstocks) on same. We saved $410 off the verified regular price! Stunning! And astonishing! $1299 for the pair. You can't make this stuff up.

Hence, purchase of the original target w/d appliance?

Didn't happen.

<u>Six weeks later</u>

It turned out that the review "best stackable" was bogus and Consumer Reports® suggested another brand, $1549 for the pair, so the first order (thankfully delayed by the infamous COVID-19 supply chain snafu) was cancelled. Furthermore, the original $1299 price didn't include necessary add-ons which meant the final cost difference proved negligible. This is the kind of bonus info that keeps literally dozens of readers borrowing my books!

Perceptibly paler

That's better. Something I can work with because it indicates that some item is noticeable and in some way not as bold as something else. So we probably have two animals, vegetables or minerals to work with along with a basis for comparison.

We could be dealing with a black cat and a grey one, fresh collards and others that were forgotten in a refrigerator drawer overlong, or obsidian and basalt. Perhaps a robust young man and his aging self—a shadow of the muscular stripling once he was. Then again a red, red rose and a pink. Emerald as versus aquamarine?

Nor must both be in the same category. A black cat and an old man, a pumpkin and a T-bolt, a lump of coal and a petunia?

The possibilities are approximately endless but its time for me to buckle in and fly this baby.

Freida Grosner lives just up the hill from me and was long a resident when I rolled in 10 years ago this month. (My, how time flies.) We often chat when she's headed down to the Saturday tailgate market in the university parking lot. She knows everyone in the neighborhood and is a seemingly endless source of local history.

She remembers the Stevensons who inherited the house across from mine and let it go to ruin before they fled, on the lam after some minor crime—she thinks that caper involved stolen ice cream and the truck it rode in on. The city finally condemned the building and the fire department burned it down, dousing and relighting multiple times for practice. The lot sat vacant for years.

There was that eccentric former news photographer with a greenhouse so overgrown that it suggested that stage play, "You know, 'Little Shop of Horrors?' It really seemed possible that something in there would gobble you up." Freida shook her head. "Scary!"

Two doors down a fellow named Tomlinson poured a ton of money into refurbishment of a 50-year-old frame house. "He put in radiant heat in a new concrete floor in what had been a dirt floor basement, new roof, new windows and foam insulation pumped into the walls. He spent a fortune, then his business went bust in the '08 recession and the bank foreclosed. Sad."

Come to think of it, all of her stories seem to include bad news. Heart attack there, divorce over here, child died in a plane crash, pit bull attacked a mail carrier, tree fell on a roof, mud slide swallowed a car. Sort of a local Cassandra, and as with that storied alarmist all of her tales have proved true.

Then she got to my house.

She told me that the previous resident had a reputation a mile wide for carousing. "One night he was good and drunk and backed into a telephone poll about half a mile from here, cracking the post and knocking his chrome bumper halfway off the rear. It dragged on the pavement all the way back home. It left a trail in the asphalt the police had no trouble following."

I shook my head. "That's pretty bad."

"Oh," she replied, "It gets worse. You know that 6 foot tall stone retaining wall between your front yard and the back?"

I nodded.

"He had driven right over it and landed down the hill. I guess he was wearing a seat belt since he didn't go through the windshield."[248]

"A year or so before you got here they found him dead. Suicide. In one of the upstairs bedrooms.[249] Nobody wanted to buy a house with that reputation and the builder who flipped it to you got it for a song." [I, however, did not.]

But enough of her stories, what of this woman, this teller of tragic tales?

Well she's a good bit younger than me and works as a legal secretary in a law firm downtown. One of the lawyers in that firm is running for a judgeship and there's a pretty good chance she'll be working for the county after the next election. (My aunt did that and followed her patron all the way to the federal bench.)

She tends to wear muted colors, I suppose reflecting the conservative taste of most of those who sort out the world's legal woes. Her reading runs to historical fiction and her film habit to documentaries. She drives a sensible beige sedan and always does the speed limit. Her cat is named Little Grey and is both. Tea not coffee. White wine not whiskey. White rice, white bread. Oatmeal not granola. [Perceptibly paler is the verdict.]

So you are going to be every bit as surprised as I was about the following drama. Marylou Esterhazy who lives four doors over

---

248 This is the verifiably true part of this story.
249 Ditto.

from me is close to Freida and the two vacationed in Spain several years ago. Marylou is many things Freida is not: loud, laughing, colorful, slapdash—and drives a bright yellow rag-top MGB-GT®. Also, whiskey *as well as* wine.

I had her over for drinks a while back and when she loosened up a bit she leaned toward me and said, "If you can keep a secret I have a hilarious story to share with you."

I assured her that I could comply.

"Are you sure? I mean, I know you're a writer and I know how writers are."

She went ahead and told me (gasp!). I'm not about to break my word so I'm going to use ellipses (...) for her part of the convo.

"..."

"When you were in Madrid?"

"..."

"And you met the man *en una taberna?*

"..."

"How much did she drink?"

"..."

"Wow, that doesn't sound like the Freida I know."

"..."

"On the table? I've heard of that, but Freida?"

"..."

"To *his* hotel?"

"..."

"The next morning?"

"..."

"..."

"That's wild!"

Later I found out that Marylou had pretty much told every adult on our mountain and sworn them all to secrecy, meaning, I think, that while she is close enough to Freida to go on vacay with her, she isn't what I would call a *good* friend.

I was only tipped off because Geoff—another neighbor—and I were talking over the fence when Freida was headed to the market one Saturday. We both waved as she passed. Then he asked, "Did you ever hear about her little wild time in Spain?"

I feigned ignorance and he relayed the story the way he'd heard it from Nancy, his wife. That version was perceptibly paler than Marylou's, though Geoff was under the impression that Freida had spent *two nights* shacked up.

(!)

"In the town where I was born"[250]

While that seems a promising start I never "lived" in the town where I was born except for however long Mom and I were in the hospital following my birth, a detail never offered to me in ensuing years. Given that her ashes have long since traveled from a stream near here to the French Broad, the Tennessee, the Mississippi and the Gulf of Mexico it seems a bit late to ask.

So if there was a man in that burg who "sailed to sea" it seems highly unlikely that he ever told *me* anything. However we can *pretend* that he told someone else. But what? And who?

Odds are that he told a woman. As we've seen, men don't talk about feelings with other men, they talk about quantum mechanics.[251] On the flip side, we've noted that men are more prone to heartbreak and heartache than women.[252] *Ipso facto*[253] if Tommy Blair had some guts to spill, he would unquestionably have spilt them to a lady.

And isn't that a strange phrase? I mean "spilt guts" must look a lot like *machaca*.[254]

To be empathetic for just a few minutes (I mean face it, I'm a guy and most guys have issues with empathy, so a few minutes is a *very* significant concession), Tommy has had more that his share of lover's knots, in both senses. No three. Well, mostly in two.

There's the one that's better known as a fisherman's knot, useful for securely fastening hooks. Then there's the interlocking loop knot that supposedly represents the intertwining of two as one—kind of a wedding thing. Finally there's the stomach tied up in knots over worry or jealousy, say when a sailor is far away and wondering if the apple of his eye has rolled further from the marital tree than he'd precisely prefer. (Some, of course, "prefer.")

We'll set aside, for now, the obvious tension between a knot

---

250 Quoting the Beatles® both dates me and adds a bit of literary polish, *non?* ("Yellow Submarine," on the album *Revolver*, Capitol®, 1966.)
251 See page 68.
252 See page 22.
253 Latin! (Or, more accurately, New Latin.)
254 *Español!* See pages 101 & 103.

used to secure a hook and another said to represent a felicitous conjoining—the one employed to facilitate an unwary "catch" while the other portraying a loving confluence—all the difference in the world there.

But the "stomach tied up in," there's the rub. As noted in the powerful disquisition about fishing and sailors in the not-to-be-missed adventure "Tied up in knots,"[255] it is a well known fact that sailors often fear that their loved ones at home are behaving in ways similar to themselves either below decks or in foreign ports. Of course, in that fascinating exploration of the psychology of atomic missile submariners, there was the added tension provided by the very stark understanding that if those sailors were ever called upon to do what they were sent out to do it was more than likely that their homes, located near their home bases, would be ground zero for an enemy nuke. Hot flashes indeed.

Also there was the possibility of implosion at great depth, an occurrence that squares the circle of "the quick" and "the dead." [You'll just have to buy the book and read the story.]

Be that as it may, Tommy was a fisherman, not a submariner, and the sea he sailed was actually a lake, albeit a very large one. You see, I was born in Oak Park, immediately adjacent to Chicago, so our protagonist, with whom we are trying to empathize—though our patience is wearing a bit thin about now—presumably boated on Lake Michigan.

Duly noted: Yes, he qualifies as a "fisherman;" i.e. he fishes, but he is not a careerist. He is a hobbyist. While he often spends a full Saturday on the lake, he doesn't sail off for weeks at a time, trawling for whatever they trawl for in a Great Lake, assuming they still trawl for things there, (likely not smelt, given what we learned on page 50), and carousing in foreign ports.

But here's the thing—and oh how our hearts go out to poor Tommy—the whole while he's pursuing his pleasure he worries that Fran might be pursuing pleasures of a different sort in his absence. How would he know? How would we?

Lord knows[256] he has tried to interest his lady love in fishing but she didn't bite, though he tried a variety of baits: Wine not beer, Coppertone® for an attractive tan, Taylor Swift® not Metallica®, even soothing a fevered brow? This confounds Tommy. How could anyone not enjoy sitting patiently in a boat, worm on a hook, beer in hand, rocking gently on the waters, not

---

255 In the fabulous collection *Waist Not, Want Knot,* BUB, 2020.
256 Coming from an atheist you realize this is tongue in cheek.

to mention soothing ones fevered brow? He's come at this six ways from Sunday[257] and the only possibility that stands out in his mind is that it must involve sex, that being the sole activity he enjoys more than angling.[258] [At least slightly.]

We haven't had a general rule for a while, so this is probably as good a time as any.

General Rule #9: "People generally assume that others share their motivations. They are generally wrong."

In the present case we don't know any more about what Fran is up to while Tommy is out to sea—which others among us might deem "out to lunch," given that he *could* spend his Saturdays with his lady love instead of squandering gas and time and, obviously, money (boat, bait, beer, gear) on a hit-or-miss effort to hook up with an unwary vertebrate which may well be too toxic for safe consumption—than he.

If her possible clandestine Saturday activity is so gut wrenching, why not park the boat and spend some quality time at home with the little lady? Why not, indeed?

Well, that's the other thing. Yes, he loves her. Yes, he's made a vow (sickness, health, poverty, wealth, having and holding 'til death dissevers, etc.). But, like many of us, he is loathe to completely sacrifice his independence. Fishing is a signifier. He angled before he wed and he will damn well angle now that he's entangled. This is the man he was, is now the man he is and will be the man he will be, venturing out alone to the deep in a small craft. Buffeted by wind and waves. Pitting his wit against critters possessing what are more knots of ganglia than brains. A man and the sea! [Not "old" as in Hemingway®—also an Oak Park native!] (I'm writing this on a Sunday morning,[259] so we can now revisit Tommy's yesterday.)

After loading his Boston Whaler® on the trailer, ending his day as a sailor and mulling his Mailer®,[260] Tommy drove to a

---

257 On Saturdays whilst rocking on the waters.
258 Suggesting that a hot'n'steamy may be just around the corner!
259 4 December, 2022
260 "The natural role of the twentieth-century man is anxiety," *The Naked and the Dead,* Rinehart & Company®, 1948. While the inclusion of Norman Mailer® was obviously due to my love of rhyme, I feel the quote is apt, both suggesting a bit of literary awareness on the part of our protagonist and opening the question of whether this also applies to 21st century men—or humans writ large—assuming Mailer® was using the then-standard "man" to express the full breadth of humanity.

lakeside bar that caters to fisherfolk and provides parking for those sailors with Whalers® on trailers. The barmaid is a longtime confidant for our boy—as also to anyone who buys a few drinks, tips well and wants to chat.

Tommy settled on a bar stool and ordered a shot of bourbon.

"Any luck?" Stacy asked.

"A couple of walleyes."

"Aren't they toxic?"

"Catch and release."

" How's Fran?"

The fisherman didn't answer immediately, knocking back the shot before replying. [Here comes the *machaca*.] "I wish I knew."

"What's with that?"

"I dunno what she does all day when I'm out on the lake."

"What do you think she does?"

"I dunno. But I wonder if she's runnin' around on me."

"Another?" Then Stacy pats his arm. "Why do you think that? Does she text while you're watching a game or something?"

"Sure, another." He shook his head. "For one thing, she never wants to go out on the boat with me. For another, sometimes she's not home when I put in after a day on the lake. For another, if she were the one out fishing and I were the one staying put I'd be bed-hopping in a New York minute."

Stacy winked. "Don't think you'd have any shortage of volunteers." She laughed. (You can see she's thinking "tip" here.)

Tommy grinned for a moment, but then, "So I worry."

"Have you thought of security cameras?"

"I couldn't do that. We're married. I have to trust her."

"And you don't."

"True. But cameras would tip her off and she'd just go to a motel or something."

"How about *not* fishing some Saturday and casing things out?"

"I couldn't do that, I have to trust her." Pause. "Besides, she might catch me."

"Private eye?"

"Too pricey."

"Well hon, maybe you just have to change the things you can and live with the things you can't, you know, like grandma's needlepoint said, 'and pray for the wisdom to know the difference.' Another?"

Tommy sipped this last one. Stacy was off dealing with other customers for a bit. When she returned, he said, "You know Stace, I'm lucky to have you to bounce ideas off. You've really helped me sort things out." He dropped cash on the bar, overpaying by at least 10 bucks. "See you next Saturday."

Meanwhile Fran was making the bed, taking a shower and fixing supper while she waited for Tommy to come home.

No telling how the bed got mussed.[261]

Note: Norman Mailer® was born in Long Branch, New Jersey, demonstrating that not *all* major writers have begun the beguine in Oak Park.

---

[261] For those among you who've been anxiously hankering for another "hot'n'steamy," just use your imagination. She *might* be having an affair with that guy she met at the gym. Greg, I think. Anyway, Norman told us we're all preternaturally anxious and here's your chance to let your freak flag fly! How do *you* think the bed got mussed? Make it lurid as you like. First time? One of many? Only Greg? Or just the regular marital muss? I can wait.

Into each life ...

This one is obvious enough, having just come in from the rain after walking a friend's dog. But isn't that a weird reference?

"Some rain must fall"—as if that is a bad thing? This goes back to the Ink Spots® who put a song together around the idea in 1944, but they swiped the idea from Henry Wadsworth Longfellow® who first penned it in "The Rainy Day"—a full century earlier—a poetic wallow in gloom and depression.

My surmise is that Longfellow was no gardener as I regard any rain short of a 500 year flood event with profound gratitude. I am much more likely to feel inklings of depression during a drought, though truth be told (and we've seen how important truth is to me) I don't think I've ever been clinically depressed.

Oh, sure, a little let down when I miss the short list for the National Book Award®, but who wouldn't be?

Depression or not, Longfellow was writing for a lot *simpler* audience which *loved* his fables about Paul Revere and Hiawatha. Then there was that ghoulish Hesperus business where a captain lashes his daughter to the mast to insure her drowning in the closing stanzas of the poem. Oh boy, *that's* amusing. [What Hollywood® might do with that today. *Titanic* watch out!]

But my attention has obviously drifted. We wandered in here to follow Megan McGilley, a mail carrier with the USPS®. She clearly knows what drops into each life—a box at a time. Unlike Mr. Longfellow she attaches no emotion to the drops, other than, perhaps, a smile when an envelope bears exterior salutations regarding a birthday, an anniversary, a graduation or a fest.

Like most couriers who brave snow, rain, heat and gloom of night while completing their appointed rounds Megan is pretty stoic. Oh, sure, unlike the carriers of yore who hoofed it from dawn to dusk she drives a trucklet, but there's still a good bit of traipsing involved in those grandfathered neighborhoods where street-side boxes are not yet required. There she often meets her clientele as she steps up on a porch to deposit the daily junk mail.

"Hi, Howard, how's the garden going?"

"Good afternoon Peggy, is Patches' leg getting better?"

"Jimmy, is that your new car?"

And so forth, demonstrating that she is woven into the social fabric hereabouts. She could have stepped out of a Norman Rockwell® *Saturday Evening Post*® cover illustration, except that back in the day the postmen were all post*men*.

[I don't think she's shattered a glass ceiling *yet* but she is part of knocking down some doors—certainly knocking *on*.]

Last month Megs was depositing a few bills and a wad of junk into Leonard Varnio's door-side box when she heard a muffled shout from inside. Something like, "Mmmf unh ggggh mmph ocht mmf unnh." (This is my best approximation of what Megs later described to me regarding the sounds.)

She said, "Leonard, is that you?"

The response was immediate. "Unh mmf ocht mmf unnh!"

"Are you alright?"

"MMF OCHT MMF!"

Well, it was clear enough that things were not alright, or at least not "normal." Megs tried the door which was unlocked and gingerly stepped in. Having gone house to house for several years she had clear memories of hankypanky scenes glimpsed behind partially open shades and knew not to judge. But this seemed different.

And it was! There was Leonard, naked, bound hand and foot with duct tape, his mouth so-sealed as well!

But still. There was the possibility this was consensual. Were Leonard and Mabel just enjoying some kinky fun?

"Are you OK?"

"Mmf nnh gggh ocht umph."

Meg leaned down and removed the tape from the man's mouth. She ripped it off in one smooth swoosh, knowing that it was bound to hurt less than a slow peel, particularly depending on the subject's recent history with a razor. An unshaved face was sure to render such ripping more painful.

"Thank God!" were Leonard's first words.[262] "I've been here since midnight."

"Where's Mabel?"

"Visiting her sister in Louisville."

"So she isn't involved?"

"What?"

"I mean, at first blush this looks like it could have some sort of S&M overtones. I don't like to interfere with someone else's

---

262 Like all of my protagonists Varnio is an atheist, but even atheists will revert to such expressions in extremis.

idea of a good time."

"I was robbed!" the alleged victim exclaimed.

Meg did some quick thinking. This was evidently a crime scene, and rule number one, actually approaching the gravity of a General Rule, is that crime scenes should not be disturbed before the "authorities" have a shot at forensic examination.

"Please un-tape me," Leonard pleaded.

"Gosh, I don't know."

"What?"

"I mean, this is evidently a crime scene and I was reflecting in the third paragraph on this page that it is almost a General Rule that crime scenes should not be disturbed before they are subjected to forensic analysis."

"But only 'almost,' right?"

"Right."

"So please, please untape me. I really have to go."

"You mean, like go to the bathroom."

"What else do you think I mean? Go to the store? Go roller-blading? Go to Europe? For God's sake,[263] untape me before I piss all over the damn carpet."

Megs considered this for few more moments, then sighed and said, "Well okay. But if this throws off the investigation, don't blame me." Then, "Hold it, I better take some photos." She pulled out her cell phone and snapped a few then pulled out a pocket knife, cut through the bindings and ripped away the tape, this time jerking out a considerable swatch of hair on the victim's ankle.

"Ouch!" This was followed by Leonard's swift exit down the hall. When he returned he was clad in a bathrobe. "Thank God you showed up!"[264]

"Oh, I always do. Snow, rain, heat, gloom ... the works. What happened?"

"That neighbor kid. You know the one who might die driving a stolen car in another year or so?"[265]

"Oh, right. I read about him in Bothwell's 2021 book. The idea was that he could still mend his ways."

"One and the same. He robbed me!"

"I guess he hasn't mended, but I think you mean he

---

263 See footnote 262.
264 Ditto.
265 Ralph Happler, in the story "Unyielding," in the utterly thrilling collection *Cede Catalogue: giving it all away*, BUB, 2021.

allegedly robbed you. Innocent until proven guilty you know."

"Alleged hell! He jumped me when I was coming out of the shower."

"Ah. I wondered why you were naked. Why didn't he just rob you while you were washing your hair?"

"He slammed me to the floor and had my wrists wrapped before I knew what was happening. Like calf roping at a rodeo."

"But he *didn't*."

"Didn't what?"

"Rope your calves. He did your ankles."

"I think he enjoyed doing me up with duct tape. He was humming the whole time."

"So, he *allegedly* enjoyed it. What did he steal?"

"How would I know? I was taped up."

"How did you land by the front door?"

"I scootched from the bedroom."

"If I were you I'd figure that out before I'd call the police. It needs to be serious or they won't even bother coming out."

"But he *duct-taped* me. If you hadn't shown up I could have died or at least peed on the carpet ."

"How's that going to look to a cop? You were allegedly taped but now you aren't. He allegedly may have taken something but you don't know what. They'll wonder if you and the Happler kid weren't just cosplaying. Was he wearing a mask?"

"An N-95."

"Hmm. Didn't think of him as that careful. Anyway give me your phone number and I'll text you the photos."

Soon our valiant carrier went on about her appointed rounds.

What she didn't expect was being called in to the station as a witness. She was questioned by Newsome and Pronke, both having been promoted to Detective rank since we last met. They've really perfected their good cop/bad cop shtick over the years and this was fully evident as they grilled our dauntless carrier. First came the cordial "Ms. McGilley" and sympathy for her weather impacted profession, then out came the 300 watt flood lamp, the Diehard® with the wires and alligator clips, the rusty pliers and the "Nice fingernails you've got there ..." squeak, squeak. "It'd be a shame if ..."

When she was suitably shaken the questions poured out. "Do you take a lot of pictures of naked men bound up in duct tape? Are mail carriers supposed to go into homes uninvited? What about female carriers? Were you and Varnio having a little hot'n'steamy while the wife was away? How long have you been dropping in to see Lenny anyway? Did you see him scootch? Did you enjoy it? Don't you know it almost approaches the gravity of a General Rule to not disturb a crime scene antecedent to forensic examination?"

Megs was in shock and could hardly mumble any answer.

"Antecedent?" She wondered, do real cops really talk that way?

Finally, "OK, you can go now. But don't leave town. We may need to interview you again."

This was followed by a solicitous farewell from the other as he doused the lamp. "Ms. McGilley you've been a tremendous help. It's citizens like you who make the American system of justice great! We can't thank you enough!"

It was about three weeks later that Meg was depositing greetings from the new dentist in town, offers for lawn service and ads for replacement windows in the Jefferson's box, about four doors down from the Varnio household. As she clapped the cover down a voice came from inside the home.

"Mmmf unh ggggh mmph ocht mmf unnh."

Meg raised her eyebrows, pursed her lips, and very quietly headed back to her trucklet as the first drops of an approaching thunderstorm began to splat in the roadside dust.

The week that wasn't

I'm feeling pretty exuberant just now for reasons I am not presently free to disclose. If all goes as planned, actually practically "promised," it will clearly redound to my benefit. If the eventuality eventuates before I slide down to the end of this motley assemblage you can be sure it will be blared all over the published cover. So check it out! (Or not. As might happen.)

Meanwhile my ebullience suggests that it is time for another General Rule. What will it be? General Rule #10 is an important one in a civilization ruled by upright beings with a corresponding number of digits (as versus mattresses which would have to use binary math, being digit-free). (The same will apply to General Rule #20 if we get that far before falling off the edge of this flat object: laptop, Kindle®, book, mattress, etc.)

General Rule #10: Um. Ah, got it! "You never know."

Boy, that covers a lot of ground! It applies to pretty much everything, does it not? "You never, never know!"

Like, say, Gerald Fortner—you know, Gerald? Yeah, *that* Gerald. "In the news" Gerald? Last week was kind of over-the-top for old Jerry. He experienced General Rule #10 in spades. Whooie!

Oh, sure, you *think* you know, but thinking only gets you so far. Certainly he *thought* he knew. But now I see a hand up and I know *exactly* what you're going to ask: "What did he think he knew?"

What? I'm wrong? You only want a hall pass? OK. Go.

[Looks like Shelley is going to miss the good part of this story if she doesn't hurry back.]

I'm guessing that the rest of you *do* want more insight into Jerry's week, am I right? Of course I'm right.

It all began a week ago, at the beginning of the week, which seems oddly serendipitous. Why then?

It's funny how coincidence can pile atop coincidence until things don't seem coincidental at all. You know? (I mean, even if "You never know" you "know" what I'm talking about. Right?)

To be clear, Jerry and I are/were "Sunday" people as versus the "Mondays." Mondays believe that fairytale about God making stuff for six days and then sitting on his butt on Sunday. We

Sundays believe in resting on Saturday and gearing up for the coming week the day after, making *that* the beginning of the week instead of the end. All the difference in the world!²⁶⁶ [Also we can't possibly believe that the universe was created in six days. Really? Hadda been a few billion years which is somewhere in the low trillions of days. And at that point whoever was running the show would've needed a day or two off no matter whether it was Saturday or Wednesday or Friday, or, yes, even Sunday.]

So, last Sunday Jerry was planning his week. He "knew" he'd have to handle the Morgan® account on Monday and thereby clear the deck for two subsidiary consults on Tuesday: Strickland® and, hmm, I guess Werner®. Or, maybe Werner® and then Lux®. If the Morgan® deal worked out, it would probably be Werner® on Tuesday, but if there were any hiccups, then Lux®? That seems about right.

Who are Strickland® and Werner®, anyway? And what does Lux® have to do with Morgan's® potential hiccups?

As far as I know Strickland® is involved with trans-shipment of some equipment from Alteiser® to the Morgan® plant that used to belong to Lux®. It was one of those sweetener deals that local governments cook up—a property tax break promised if a company meets certain investment and hiring goals within a specified time frame.

Morgan® is a Lux® supplier, and you have to know that Lux® pulled off a major scam, right?

I mean, Lux® had benefited from a tax rebate program about 10 years ago when it bought the old Briggs & Stratton®²⁶⁷ plant over on the south side. Their expansion had earned back every penny promised to the point that they paid, essentially, no property taxes at all over that decade.

When time came to upfit the factory Lux® cooked up a deal with another city in another state and moved, leaving the local plant idle, but with Morgan® in the wings, its execs dining with local muni officials on the company tab. Soon enough Morgan® framed a sweet tax rebate deal to move into the former Lux® complex, promising big investments and new jobs.

Of course the "new" jobs would go to the same workers who'd been laid off months earlier when Lux® left. So Morgan® would get credit for hiring the "unemployed" left behind by the

---

266 But duly noted, we are *not* Seventh Day Adventists®.
267 I'm using a real corporate name to lend verisimilitude, but my legal team wants me to be clear that B&S® are not in any way involved here.

parent company. On top of that, the machine tools, metal brakes, drill presses, grinders, buffers, benders, lifts, chain pulls, and so on and so forth—that Lux® had left behind—were perfectly suited to the tasks to be handled by Morgan®. So Morgan® "bought" the old tools from Lux® and thus received credit for "new" investment in the old plant. The Alteiser® facility is also owned by Lux®. [More than one way to skin a city, as the saying goes.]

So Jerry knew he'd have some tetchy negotiations to negotiate on Tuesday. Then, if all went well, on Wednesday he'd be in talks with Gasperson Inc.®

Gasperson®, a subsidiary of Morgan®, was working a deal with the county to build housing on municipal land earmarked for economic development. The argument was that all those "new" workers who would be employed at the "new" plant would need places to live. (Of course we "know" that, in fact, the new worker-bees were actually Lux's® old worker-bees who, presumably, had some sort of housing already—except for the ones who'd been living paycheck to paycheck and who'd been evicted in the several weeks since Lux® left.

So the deal was that the Gasperson® apartments would offer Morgan® employees first dibs on units priced at 30 percent or less of their monthly wages. ("Less" was included for the benefit of local voters who bothered to pay attention. "Less" was obviously a fiction.) In exchange Gasperson® would pay no property taxes on the acreage for the first 30 years of operation.

Jerry knew that there was some opposition on the county commission so his consult on Thursday morning with the Gasperson® team was to line up the arguments he'd present to commissioners in private talks before the evening meeting when they'd presumably vote to approve the real estate deal.

If all went well Jerry "knew" that on Friday he and a handful of executives from Lux®, Morgan®, Strickland®, Werner® and probably Alteiser®, would be celebrating with a round of golf and a few rounds of drinks, followed by a banquet at the local country club. He *"knew"* this would be the capstone deal of his negotiating career!

What he didn't "know" was the trajectory of the chunk of a Chinese rocket that would reenter the atmosphere early Monday morning. Pulling into that Starbucks® drive-thru was obviously the wrong move at the wrong time. "Over-the-top" indeed.[268] Right through his damn sunroof.

---

[268] See page 125.

"Distance is gone"[269]

Well. That last one was a little bleak. Poor Jerry. He just *knew* this was going to be his best week ever. I guess saving the best for last got tangled up somehow, last coming first and so on.

But what about Shelley? Did she make it back to hear the heart-stopping story? (Or spacejunk-stopping, as the case transpired.)

No.

She dawdled as she is wont to do and only heard about Jerry's *dénouement*[270] from Louise after class. Consequently she didn't get the story quite right and thinks that Alteiser® owns Lux® instead of the other way around, and that she might qualify for a new apartment in the Gasperson® complex. [No.]

It is so damn easy for misinformation to spread in these days of late-stage capitalism!

Anyway, Louise meant well and that's something. I mean to say there are some redeeming features to good intentions, road to hell or no. Significantly, I think, they make the intender feel good.

It seems we've stumbled into another General Rule!

General Rule #11: "Good intentions make the intender feel good."

There are probably other pleasant spin offs, but now we're talking about Louise, bless her heart.[271]

Why she's been sitting in on my philosophy class is anybody's guess. I mean, I don't care that she's not enrolled, and I'm confident that exposure to my examination of what we think and what ensues will obviously benefit any "thinking" person. Auditing my instructional effort is bound to be edifying, and if <u>enough of you</u> (hint, hint) do that the world will gradually become a better place: i.e. universal single payer, rational minimum wage, higher taxes on corporations and the wealthy, and so on and so forth.

---

269 From the Moody Blues®, "The Best Way to Travel," *In Search of the Lost Chord,* Deram Records®,1968

270 Note how much more final this sounds *en français*, as indicated by the accent gravé.

271 South of the Mason/Dixon this phrase is a pejorative. But she's OK.

Louise is a paralegal.

Yes, she's involved in matters of the law like so many of the characters in my sometimes outlandish fiction. There are the lawyers attending cross examination of clients by Newsome and Pronke, the lawyer who fell in and out of love with a French fraud, the one who steered Patsy the painter through a messy divorce, the lawyer for whom my neighborhood Cassandra labors and many more. [You can read all of my many short story collections to meet every one of them up close and personal! So go!]

Here's a thing, if not *the* thing: In high school I imagined I wanted to be a lawyer! I joined a Boy Scout® Explorer® group focused on becoming a future legal eagle. Fortunately I was bored out of my wits and dropped the idea like a hot rock before the end of my junior year.

That's "a" thing. But "the" thing didn't hit me for about forty years. In the mid-aughts I was dating a lawyer and what I inferred is what I missed all those decades ago. Lawyers are always stuck in the middle between people who aren't happy with circumstances or each other. What a miserable place to be! No matter the outcome, someone involved—and very likely everyone—will be at least disappointed if not outright angry with you.

Oh sure, you got the murderer a life sentence instead of death but "life" in the joint isn't really happy making, you got or lost a settlement in an insurance fraud case and still got your fee, you sued and gained or failed in a libel suit which left all participants feeling a little besmirched, and so much more.

On the other hand, we all manage to be lawyerly a lot of the time in the sense that we engage in *post hoc*[272] justification. Once we've done something, however misguided, it is remarkably easy to land on very good reasons for the doing. We believed someone else, we imagined that was a good plan, we were drunk, and oh—a biggie—the end justified the means! Don't blame me!

Louise, of course, is spared the worst of it, only being a para-. That's more clerical than fisticuffs. But she still has to listen to the whiny attorneys lamenting everything except their trips to the bank or Cancun.

Fortunately Louise is a tough nut. She can handle the lamentations with sympathetic nods and "oh mys" and not take any of it to heart. You see, she is a genuinely happy person with a *life of her own* that isn't attached to what she does Monday through Friday, 8 a.m. to 4—except as fiscal underpinning.

---

[272] Latin!

She and her wife Gwendolyn have a nice little cottage with a nice little garden and nice little cats, the epitome of wedded bliss. They are film buffs and watch nice little films noir from the 40s and 50s into the nice little wee hours on weekends and often into the less wee—but still nice—hours on weeknights. The cynicism expressed in those flicks is so much more fun than the commercial cynicism Louise sees daily in the office! The loving couple cuddle and quip as the (mostly) black and white dramas unreel.

But this story is really about Gwendolyn, not Louise, and certainly not the dawdling Shelley.

Gwen is the daughter of circus performers. [I bet you didn't see *that* coming!] She grew up with stage paint and juggling, walks a high wire with the best of them, has tamed a lion or two in her time, and even helped erect the big top in cities across the country. She can tell you *that's* a major feat!

Then how, pray tell, did she meet Louise? The carney life and the staidly clerical seem widely spaced.

Well, well. The idea of running away to join the circus is a lamentably over-worn trope in fiction—a trope, that is, in the sense of a phrase that stands in for something else. As a f'rinstance: going AWOL from the military to seek one's fortune as a placer miner in Alaska could be so characterized. Or dropping out of college to try one's luck with crypto currency. See?

But how often do we hear about people who <u>run away from the circus?</u> Hmm? Well now we have.

One day Gwen was simply fed up with the travel, the low pay, the non-stop performances, the low pay, the groping by clowns, the low pay, and etc. Also the low pay. She ducked under the canvas and sprinted off, never looking back.

Oh there were some rough months, sleeping under bridges, standing in food lines at shelters, dealing with bad behavior among other street people or the cops and not having a good shot at a hot shower and a warm bed. But she was free! Free at last!

Then one afternoon she was staring up at the marquee on an arthouse theater with a wistful look on her besmudged visage. *Angels With Dirty Faces*—a 1938 Michael Curtiz® classic—was showing as part of a local film festival. Louise stepped up to the box office and noticed Gwen's sadly plaintive look.

"You here to see the show?"

Gwen shook her head. "Would love to. Can't afford it."

"It's only $8."

"I'm about seven and change shy."

"You a major fan? Of noir?"

"More than major. Super major. Super-duper major.""

"I'll buy you a ticket."

"You sure? I may not be an angel (she winked with just a hint of sexual insinuation) but you doubtless noticed my dirty face."

"I don't judge books by covers and, hey, you're kind of hot."

And so the two watched the film and hit a nearby cafe for espresso afterward (coffee noir?). Louise learned a good bit about Gwen's trajectory and was particularly sympathetic regarding the shower problem. She invited her new friend over for the night.

Scrubbed and combed-out Gwen was a new person. Soon they were laughing in pajamas and then shared a bed,[273] given that Louise had only the one in her apartment. Over breakfast they laughed some more until Louise turned serious.

"What's next my friend?"

"Back on the street. Something will come up. I really appreciate what you've given me. This has been kind of magical."

"Look. I can't see you doing that. Stay here. You'll find a job or something and we can figure things out. This apartment isn't much but it's a place to land."

"I can't do that. You've already done more for me than anyone in months."

"You *can* do that. This. Get your feet under you again."

"Oh, Louise. I don't know what to say."

"Try 'yes.' I've got to go to work, but throw your clothes in the washer and make yourself at home. I'll be back about 5."

They hugged before our paralegal's departure. Gwen was a little teary-eyed. "Oh, Louise."

Well, as you can certainly imagine, one thing led to another.[274] Gwen soon found work as an instructor at a local clown school, helping to encourage folks who aim to run away. Two years later when the Supreme Court came around they married, and another couple of years in they bought the cottage.

It seems in this case, at least, that good intentions worked out pretty well. Louise entertained no ulterior motive though that wink—*that wink*. Gwen was purely wishing to see a film. But she *did wink*. Two women from relatively remote parts of our society are now peas in a noirish pod, the distance having gone.

---

273 Note: this is *not* a hot'n'steamy. Strictly *phillia*. But soon. *Soon!*
274 Note: this *is* a hot'n'steamy.

Next question: "Will we find out?"[275]

---

[275] From the Moody Blues®, "The Best Way to Travel," *In Search of the Lost Chord,* Deram Records®,1968

"Will we find out?"[276]

It looks like we left our dawdler out of most of the previous tale, so what's up with Shelley? (That would work with the title upstairs, wouldn't it??? Will we? Find out?)

Back when Shels was missing my incisive lecture and before Louise filled her in to some degree on my thesis, she was somewhere down the hall reading flyers tacked on a bulletin board—a wide expanse of *"Lost Dogs and Mixed Blessings"*[277] as John Prine®—RIP—framed things. The mix included band promotions, roomie wanted, used textbooks at a discount, help wanted, job wanted, thespian tryouts, bike for sale, and, yes, a missing pup.

:-(← Sad face. I'm still working on that graphic book nom'.

What really caught her eye, however, was a notice regarding a fledgling book club.[278] (Shelley, as you may not be aware, is a keen reader in addition to being a preternatural dawdler.) The organizing theme of the club just aborning was to be "authors who have yet to be shortlisted for the National Book Award®."

This intrigued Shelley (how many could there be?) and she added the contact number to the notepad on her cell.

After class (which she had stealthily reentered just before the closing bell) and after walking down the quad with Louise during which walk the latter more or less explicated the business dealings of Lux®, et. al., Shels phoned and left a message. "I want to read!" she exclaimed.

Following a call back she put the following Wednesday evening on her cell calendar, with an alert scheduled for two hours ahead in case she was busy dawdling. In the meantime she purchased and read a used copy of *Seize You on the Dark Side of the Moo*,[279] a mind-boggling collection of tales by the professor whose recent class she had dawdled past. Small world! (She made sure to place her copy atop her desktop stack of books at the next session of the philosophy course, hoping to boost her grade.)

[I am not *that* easily bought off, by the way. See page 97. I

---

276 See footnote 275.
277 Prine's® 12th album issued by Oh Boy®, 1995.
278 See "Book Club Discussion Questions" at the rear end of this mess.
279 BUB, 2019

am, of course, pleased to know she is a reader. Shelley really needs to up the ante if she wants a better grade. Maybe study?]

But here's the thing (and I just know—I mean even if General Rule #10 applies—that you are eager to *know* the "thing") that happened on Wednesday night.

Shelley met Randy! Randy!

You can just *imagine* how that changed everything!

Later that night Shels couldn't fall asleep. So many of the things Randy had said echoed in her mind.

"A talking steer is preposterous," he'd observed. And, "What kind of electrician would own a goat dairy?" Then, repeating, "A goat dairy?"

Randy seemed so *deep!* Oh, gosh, she hoped he felt the same connection she felt! Next Wednesday couldn't come soon enough!

We'll be extra nice to her and sort of speed things up here, so it won't take *absolutely forever* for the week's events to transpire, dawdling or no.

Let's see. Thursday she told Louise (who is still auditing my class, whatever) that she'd met a really dreamy guy at her first book club meeting. Dreamy and deep.

Louise said she was happy for Shels. "Congrats. But a guy?"

Then, later that day, she dawdled a good bit.

Um, Friday ... what happened Friday? Oh, right, Louise had to go to the county courthouse to look up some records for one of the legal eagles at her firm. While all of the current and recent docs are available online, the local government is still wading through old records to digitize them. It's going to take a while.

One of the problems involved is that young employees were never taught cursive in school what with longhand falling out of favor. This renders many older documents illegible to today's young adults.

There's a spirited debate going on regarding the importance of that change in education. Some argue that most writing these days is digital, either typed or dictated and that the ability to read, say, the Declaration of Independence® (in its original form) is of no particular utility. After all, most documents that are deemed to matter have long ago been available in print form. Others assert that something essential is being lost. For example those letters from your great-grandmother that the family has preserved down through the years, written by her hand and full of her love for her progeny. You won't find that on Google®. Nay, nay.

But back to Shel's story. Friday she went to two classes and chilled all afternoon doing a mental "he loves me/he loves me not" with an imaginary flower. (Always with an odd number of petals. She is mathematically attuned.)

Saturday was a great day for dawdling it seems, and Shels took full advantage. The day felt springlike, a warm bump in the otherwise chilly fall, and she dawdled her way across campus and down to the brook that bounds the grounds. There she sat on a favorite smooth boulder, relaxing in the sun and reading another too often overlooked, un-shortlisted treasure, *Lucky Breaks (breaking good)*.[280]

Wasn't it true, she thought, that discontinuity often led to positive outcomes? Why, just think (she thought) ... if she hadn't broken with habit last Wednesday, and had therefore missed the first meeting of the book club, she'd never have met Randy!

"What kind of electrician would own a goat dairy?" Indeed!

The rock was sun-warm and the book just a little boring and before she knew it she was napping, only to awaken an hour or so later when voices interrupted her reverie.

Two other students had wandered to creekside and were just around a bend, out of sight but clearly audible.

"The problem, as I see it, is that she's a dawdler."

"Well, yeah, but ..."

"But what?"

"Well, she's gorgeous."

"What does that have to do with anything?"

"What doesn't it have to do with?"

"Weren't we talking intellect?"

"She's easy on the eyes is what I'm saying."

"That and 5 bucks will get you a mocha latte."

"If I had 5 bucks I'd buy her one."

The voices gradually faded as the speakers evidently walked downstream.

Who could they have been talking about?

The day was cooling at that point and Shels headed back to the dorm.

Sunday was much chillier, as a cold front had moved in overnight, so Shels dawdled indoors, visiting the college art collection and then settling in a study carrel in the library to continue her reading. Oh, and doodling. Like many another dawdler she doodles, doodling being a near relative of dawdling.

In her case the resulting depictions are less random than

---

280 BUB, 2022.

the usual jottings of a run-of-the-mill non-directional doodler. Her mother had introduced her to "wiggle pictures" when she was a youngster. Of course she also drew hearts, particularly now that she couldn't get Randy out of her mind, but the wiggles were more creative.

Normally "wiggle pictures" were initiated as a shared activity with first one and then the other making a seemingly random bit of scrawl, usually with a ballpoint or felt-tip pen, so that erasure was not an option. Then the other would use that start to depict something tangible. Here's an example.

You see on the left the initial wiggle, then on the right the drawing made from the wiggle by the other participant. (Hint: the wiggle on the left became the girl's nose. Try this at home!) Duly noted, Shelley was doing a solitaire version between short stories.

Oh, Sunday night she watched a movie, *Love Story*, considered one of the most romantic films ever made. It left her in tears. Oh, so tragic! And yes, Shels agreed, "Love means never having to say you're sorry.[281] Oh, yes. Yes. And dying is so *romantic!*"

Monday Shels went into town to buy a new outfit and landed at Spiritex®[282] where she purchased an organic cotton jacket that really "worked" with her blue eyes and blond locks. She just *knew*, to the extent that any of us can know anything, that Randy would love it!

That night she watched *Love Story* again. [I think she was getting a little carried away, don't you?]

Tuesday Shels had a long talk with Heather after their calculus class, saying things like:

$$\frac{df}{dt} = \lim_{h \to 0} \frac{f(t+h) - f(t)}{h}$$

---

281 Reminding me of a truly terrible joke.
282 A real store in Asheville. All organic!

As previously noted Shelley is a math nerd. She can do *df/dt* like a champ! As can Heather who is aiming for a *career* in mathematics. She sees herself as a future college professor, with a double doctorate in theoretical physics and number theory, eventually leading to a Nobel®.

Shels on the other hand just thinks calculus is great fun. [Sometimes she doodles equations instead of making wiggle pictures.]

Tuesday afternoon felt interminable. After the exciting conversation with Heather the rest of the day just dragged. In fact Shelley was too bored to dawdle! Oh dear! When would Wednesday arrive? Doodle, doodle, doodle.

Arrive it did! Just after midnight! But then she had to sleep, wanting to be fit and fresh for the evening discussion, and she slept in until almost 9 a.m. (!)

Shels could hardly concentrate during her Psych 102 class, and was little better in Spanish 103. All she could think about, really, was Randy. Randy, Randy, Randy.

She dressed up for the club meeting, in an ivory blouse, her jungle purple leggings and, obviously, her new jacket. Looking good! Way good! Way, way good!

Randy, of course, didn't show. He'd been quite serious when he commented on the title story of the book under discussion. When I saw him later in the week I asked what he thought about Shelley.

"Who?"

Too little, two late

Premonstratensian. Didn't see that coming, now did you? That'll rock anyone on their heels, I think, though I've gotta say that using "their" instead of "her" or "his" still feels kind of uncomfortable. "Their" has always been plural in my book(s) and the singular "their" feels ... I dunno ... forced. "Anyone" is singular, right? I predict it will take at least a couple <u>of</u> generations for that-there "their" to really take hold. (Am kind of sure all traditional Premonstratensians were/are men, but maybe not. Are there non-traditionals? Curious people want to know.)

Which reminds me of that other grammatical sin: "couple" sans "of." (I'll go back and underline the "of" above.) (Done.)

All manner of writers imagine they can get away with "a couple generations" instead of applying the correct usage of the combinatory frame. It is and has always been "a couple of." I mean, those "woke" grammar Nazis who are insistent on imposing the singular "their" do not have a leg to stand on (or a couple of legs, to pluralize the idiom) regarding "couple of" absent the "of." There is no measure of gender neutrality summoned regarding that "of." No social posturing. No shaming, no bullying, no judgmental twist. This is either a function of laziness on the part of writers or, to be generous, those writers using my desktop keypad on which the "F" key requires a serious pounding to register on the screen. [So we often get a "couple o" which sounds kind o' Irish.]

Now, back to our long word of the day! Premonstratensian.

Gotta say I just about fell over backward when I stumbled on that one this morning!

Like most of you I am given to reading abstruse fictions of the philosophes in the wee hours and was proceeding through a fun-filled (and kind of weird) episode from *Denis Diderot*[283] when "Premonstratensian" leapt into my hungry and drooling retinas. Ooooh! Had to read it a few times to sort of naturalize the flow. Six syllables!

The Premonstratensians were a hot mess, and maybe still are. It isn't like intense religious assemblages *evaporate*. They

---

283 Yes, *français!*

cling to existence, advocating nonsense that evidently appeals to some subset of what we might call "rational humanity." Well, no, a "formerly rational subset" seems more apt. But subset, no less.

Really. I mean, *really*. For one obvious thing, the Premos wore/wear white robes. Oh, yeah? That alone precludes any serious work. Get under the hood in a bleached burqa and you're headed for smudged and smeared gray in a hot hurry. I don't care how many "brothers" (okay, given job distribution in late capitalist—or late medieval—society, likely "sisters") are working in the steamy abbott's habit department—rather, the abbott's steamy habit house, which is not to opine that the abbott has no steamy habits, w-w/o joints, since some abbotts probably smoke pot—grease stains on a *fleur de sel* habit are not gonna come out. New and Improved Tide® or no.

So my guess is that, while they hated the Jansens, the Premos kept some supplicant Jansens on staff to change the oil and grease the wheels and generally keep the gray grime off the home team. I mean, have you ever seen a Jansen in a white shirt?

Didn't think so.

[To be clear, the Jansens are in no way connected to Jantzen®, the fabricator of garments which can probably be— sometimes at least, though not necessarily—white.] [Do wearers of achromatic Jantzen® sportswear ever get under a hood? My sense is "no."] [To be further clear I am not one to sit in judgment of Jansens who choose to work for Premonstratensians. We all need to secure a line of income. Gray area or no.]

But this little contretemps involves neither Jansens or Jantzens® but rather a pair of (see title) Johnsons, both arriving at the laundry somewhat after the opening gong (see title). The women—blood sisters as it happens—had been hired after the scrub-Jansens[284] took offense and quit. Again.

Therese and Rose have been pinch-hitting in the washhouse for several years, as the Jansen pack peeve periodically, taking their jobs and shoving them at fairly regular intervals—which I think we have to admire.

There are, after all, many among us who feel like TTJ&ESSing, but how many *do?* We are far more likely to "give notice," seeing as we will presumably need another gig at some point. "Notice" at least tempers the job references. The Jansens however would walk at the drop of a Biblical bromide, the

---

284 I have it on good authority that Premonstratensians do neither mechanical repair nor clean-up. Gotta keep those robes stain free!

dropping of which is more or less second nature to devout Premos.

One of the scrub-Jansens, a "religious" sister (as versus blood), while rubbing muslin on a washboard, would whisper to the next, "Did you hear what Andre said at vespers?"

"No, I was sitting near the back of the cloister. It's hard to hear anything clearly there. Sounds echo off the stone walls, y'know? You'd think management would do something about the acoustics if they expect us to pay attention. A few heavy tapestries would work wonders!"

"Lilies of the field."

"He said *that!*"

"Plain as day. 'Lilies of the field' indeed!"

The second woman dropped the object of her labor into the suds. "I'm gone."

"I'm with you."

Andre soon learned that all activity in the *buanderie*[285] had ceased and he sent Jerome to check on the Johnsons' availability. As expats with a comfortable inheritance the pair didn't really need work, but enjoyed experiencing "local flavor." A few days labor for the—possibly steamy—abbott now and again, flavored their carefree *émigré*[286] existence in interesting ways and provided a little mad money to boot.

Jerome found the two women seated at a *café*[287] table, drinking wine and playing cribbage beneath a wide umbrella. They were dressed alluringly, as was their usual when not working the washboards. (Not for the first time did the monk entertain second thoughts about his vow of celibacy. He'd spent many hours reading the rules, searching for a loophole in hopes that perhaps the written letter of the law might be bent regarding non-Premonstratensians—non-Premonstratensians on the order of the lovely women he now second-thoughtfully approached.)

"I am fortunate indeed to find you here on this delightful day, a pleasant afternoon nearly as lovely as the mademoiselles."

"Why, if it isn't our favorite penitent," Rose said, flashing the messenger a welcoming smile.

Therese greeted him as well. "Hello Jerome. What brings the handsomest monk in the abbey to town at this gorgeous *cock-*

---

285 Again, *français!* And, no, the Johnson sisters are not. They hale from Texas.
286 More *français!* By gosh!
287 And again!

tail hour?" [Her emphasis, not mine.]

Fully aware of his pledge the sisters were inclined to gentle torment, flirting and teasing. (Not that either was unwilling if a fish decided to bite. No one back home would know! Free birds!)

"The usual errand, which I happily perform given the recipients of my usual missive." He tipped his head in a sort of gestural bow. "The scrub-Jansens hath fled."

"Can it wait until tomorrow morning? We were just talking about taking advantage of this glorious afternoon." Therese gestured broadly.

"How so?"

"You know the pond just down the path, there off the road between here and your abbey?" Rose continued, after he nodded. "We thought to take a swim."

"That sounds refreshing."

"But there's a problem, Jerome. Perhaps you can help?"

"Happy to be of service."

"We don't have swimsuits," Therese giggled.

Jerome stammered, "And, um, how can I help?"

"Well, swimming naked is a *sensual*[288] delight as you surely know, but how would we protect our privacy? I just now thought you might guard the path while we unrobe and take a dip."

He swallowed hard. "I, um, don't see why not."

Soon enough the cribbage board was in a bag, the check was settled, and the three set off, chatting amiably as acquaintances will. Jerome was doing his best to appear calm though his mind was racing.

At the last bend on the way to the water he said, "I'll stop here. Enjoy the swim!"

"We won't be *too* long," Rose offered. "No more than half an hour *completely*[289] nude. Thanks for protecting us from prying eyes! You are a kind friend."

As the women disappeared into the greenery the monk thought hard. Was there a loophole regarding peeking? Prying? He quickly decided he barely knew (see title) enough of the law to be held accountable and very cautiously and quietly followed the bathers down toward the shore.[290] He hid behind a shrub.

Ooo-la-la, as the French are said to say. [His second thoughts turning to thirds and even fourths.]

---

288 Not *français*. Italicized here to suggest her *suggestive* pronunciation.
289 Her emphasis not mine.
290 See reference to *post hoc* reasoning on page 127.

Extirpated[2]

    I think by now you know that I try to be completely honest with you. Sure, I make up stories, but they are true stories in the best sense of either word. I know that the [2] upstairs has probably raised questions and so, being who and what I am, I will set chagrin and ego and false pride and reason aside and explain.
    This is the 35th tale in the current volume.
    See? That wasn't so hard, was it?
    We left Heather back on page 137 with career plans but else-wise sort of a cipher. What does she do when she isn't solving equations? What's her favorite color? Is she seeing someone?
    I see a hand up. Do you have a question or an answer?
    "Yes."
    Is that an answer to my previous query or the one before?
    "Both."
    Well ...
    "The answer is no. She's not. But the question is what does the 35th have to do with anything?"
    I was just getting to the one before. You're right. Heather is so set on her lofty education goals that she constrains her socialization. She's not going to risk falling in love and so on and so forth[291], eventualities that could derail her good intentions.[292]
    Um, oh, right, blue. Most people's fave.
    And, let's see. Well, for one thing, she doesn't doodle. Nor dawdle. I'm pretty sure that's what she likes about Shelley. Shels kind of covers for her. Some of the people who have unsuccessfully sought dates are inclined to think she is just <u>too damned serious,</u> but others will remind them, "Hey, she hangs with Shels. She can't be all *that* stuffy."
    Also Shels makes her laugh with calculus jokes. Calculus jokes! [Like: What did one function say to the other function? Heh, heh.]
    "Are you avoiding?"
    Avoiding?
    "The question."

---

291 "So forths" like a surprise pregnancy to name just one.
292 See General Rule #11.

No, I was about to answer. The $dy's$[293] the limit! Oh that one cracks me up!

"Very funny. No, about the 35th."

I take it you're not a reader.

"No, I'm a math major like Heather."

Oh, so *that's* how you know her. I'd guess you're one of the guys who've angled for a date. No luck I bet. If I were you I'd start on a different tangent. Tell her a few calculus jokes and she might come up with a different answer. Or a *differential* one anyway.

"The 35th?"

Kind of hung up with numbers are we? If you were a reader you'd recall that the 35th story in *Lucky Breaks*[294] was ... take a guess.

"Extirpated?"

Bingo.

"So the ² doesn't mean the value is squared."

Nope. Actually it's halved because I've used it twice. But here's a tip. If you flunk calculus like I did and decide to try your luck with short stories you can use my method. When you start in on another book ...

"Don't you have to write one in order to have another?"

Simple math there, smart ass. This tip is for the <u>next</u> one. So you will have obviously saved the first file on your laptop or your phone, wherever you do your writing. And it's already formatted, right? Because, I mean, you might as well format the thing while you're writing so you can keep track of how big the thing is going to be when it's printed. See?

I mean, if you don't decide ahead just how big the thing is going to be you'll end up with a doorstop like *Infinite Jest*,[295] a book that no one can pick up without a forklift. A reasonable book should land at about 200 pages. [Wallace® didn't ask my opinion and produced a volume 5+ times the correct length.]

Or take Rolling Stones® musician Keith Richards® who dragged on for almost 600 pages in his autobio. Trust me Keith, no one is *that* interesting.

Anyway, the second one is way easier to assemble. See? You just change the title, and the foreword (which you write *last*, after you know what the book is about), and so on. Here's the thing: You already have a table of contents! So you can just plug in the

---

293 As in *dy/dx*. Get it?
294 BUB, 2022
295 David Foster Wallace®, Little, Brown and Company®, 1996.

names of the new stories and the corresponding page numbers and then here's the <u>really big thing!</u> When you're stuck for the name of a new tale you already have the titles of the old ones to help out! I had a brief spell of writer's block when I arrived at item number 35 in the current effort. [About a minute and a half, FWIW. Actual "writer's block" is a pagan myth, IMHO] And there it was! I simply attached the ² so my baker's dozen of loyal fans would understand that it was a different story. I would hate for them to miss all this fun because they imagined they'd already read it.

Time's a-wasting and none of us wants to reread a bit of fiction we've already internalized—even if it's unbelievably brilliant and likely headed for a National Book Award®! [I endlessly reread this stuff during the editing process, to save you, my several readers, from expending any of your few remaining minutes on planet earth in the effort.] [A "thank you" would be nice right about now.]

But, back to Heather. Or, rather, back to Heather's back. Like many of today's misguided young people this woman thinks tattoos she can't see without a mirror are the cat's pajamas. [Cats, if you have failed to notice, can, in fact, see their backs. Even lick them. Limber as the dickens.]

Humans, if you have failed to notice, can't see much of their backs, let alone lick them. [Well, yeah, there are contortionists among us and just possibly a few have likely pulled off a back-lick. My sense would be "vanishingly few."]

[OMG! I just noticed it is 3:57 p.m. and time for NPR's® *All Things Considered*. I know this conflicts with my oft-mentioned practice of writing at 3:30 a.m. but I make occasional exceptions. The problem at the moment is this: If I want to maximize my return on investment regarding my monthly contribution to the local affiliate I need to turn on the radio *right now*. However if I do that I will lose my train of thought, a ticket purchased and forfeited at great price.]

[Later.] The train left the "station" when I tuned in. [Mixed metaphor or what?]

I'll get back to Heather's back in a few, but what happened to her yesterday was pretty strange. After OJ and coffee and a few bites of yogurt and a handful of blueberries she felt queasy. Really, really queasy. Then, an hour or so later, even queasier. Like, kind of "might vomit queasy." Plus a fever. A wiping-sweat-off-her-forehead sort of fever.

This wasn't helping with her calculus homework. Oh, no.

That's Life

Plus, well, I sort of think you don't want these graphic details, even in a book likely to be short-listed as a graphic novel-type affair, but she experienced what Brit readers might characterize as frequent "skips to the loo."

Then the—briefly noted—dry heaves. [Mostly dry anyway.]

Around noon the symptoms subsided. No telling. Some sort of food poisoning one must suppose. She rinsed the blueberries for whatever that's worth, as the print on the package suggested. But we note here that in January blueberries in North Carolina hale from a *foreign* nation. Suspect or what? Was Peru short of hand sanitizer in this time of cholera?

The principle value of the last few grafs is to establish a human connection with our heretofore sketchily limned student.

Who among us has not had a dry heave or two? [Inserting a "toe wiggle" here, versus raised hands. Even typing *that* triggers an involuntary movement of my southern digits.]

Her back. Tattooed as noted upslope. We've met another character so stenciled—Samantha in "One you can sink your teeth into."[296] But whereas Samantha had the sad history of her love life thus recorded, we know that Heather has avoided similar pitfalls.

Well, no. Not entirely sad. Samantha's record included the best years, with her dog, Robbie.[297] Not a pitfall! [Nor a pit bull!]

For Heather, absent any lovers, what? Equations!

Yes! Heather's epidermis sports the complete set of differential equations needed to manufacture a cellphone! Or so she thinks. She can't see the whole inscription from any angle even using a full-length mirror and a hand-held and as noted she is absent a significant other to examine her bare-naked self and read it off. She won't even let me see it and I know her about as intimately as is humanly possible. (I have *imagined* her naked.)

So the only person who has seen all of the artwork on Heather's backside is the woman who wielded the needle. While Melanie is quite creative and dressed things up with flowers and birds she is not particularly attentive to mathematical detail.[298]

If Heather is ever kidnapped by corporate raiders intent on producing cheap knock-off phones, they'll be flat out of luck. Their villainy extirpated[2!] But it would be a thrilling adventure and she'll be able to sell her story to Disney® or Pixar®.[299]

---

296 Page 42 in *Self Evident: We hold these tooths,* BUB, 2020.
297 You really need to read that story!
298 Another calculus dropout I'm afraid.
299 We are one-shy of 300 footnotes and only on page 145! A new record!

More earthworms![300]

Dave, named by the discoverer's nephew, was supposedly the world's largest known earthworm when he/she was unearthed in the U.K. in 2016. This is one of those things you just can't make up and I didn't. The little gal/guy was almost 16 inches long and "weighed as much as a bar of baking chocolate."

Why the naturalist who examined him/her came up with that comparator for Dave's weight is anybody's guess. Perhaps it was close to lunch time and her tummy was growling. I dare say most of us don't think "chocolate" when herding worms.

Dave outpaced the previous record setter, a Scottish entrant who only weighed in at half a bar.

As reported at the time by CBS News®, "Emma Sherlock, senior curator of free-living worms at the Natural History Museum® and chair of the Earthworm Society of Britain®, said that Dave's size is astounding."

Of course as we learned during our little adventure in Vietnam back in the day, if you want to save something you have to start by destroying it. Poor Dave. Euthanized and dropped in a bottle of formaldehyde to "preserve" him/her for the future.

Somehow—and do realize I don't know Ms. Sherlock or even whether she "did the deed"—it would seem that if I were a curator of free-living worms I would have settled Dave in a nice box of rich compost to find out if he/she might grow larger. Time enough for formaldehyde when the girl/boy expired. Think how much more "astounding" Dave would have been at 2 ounces and almost 3 feet long!

But here's the thing I didn't see coming when I looked up the world's largest earthworm a half hour ago,[301] and I would suppose the same is true for you. My most recent adoptee, a 12-year-old, grey tiger domestic shorthair feline was sitting in my lap at the time, and his name, no fooling, is Sherlock. Coincidence? I think not. (He arrived here two years ago with that name inscribed on his veterinary record.)

---

300 I don't have anything to add about earthworms at just this moment, but I was so excited about hitting #300 that I just had to proceed. Bingo!
301 About 8:15 a.m. EST, 7 January, 2023, or 1:15 p.m. GMT for Emma.

You can tell we're veering back into the whole matter of where ideas come from. As, for example, the title of this parable.

I had just wrapped up the previous exciting story about examining Heather's decorative if dysfunctional back-tat and was staring out the window when an early bird landed atop one of the stone arches I built several years ago. The connection with worms is self-evident, though this was a cardinal which is less associated with morning worm extraction than, say, a robin. So the universe was handing me a free title. [It keeps a person grateful.]

But what on earth led me to a search for the world's longest? Wow. That takes me back about 20 years to when I was briefly managing editor of the local newsweekly. [True fact.] A fellow who was either nuts or a superb actor knocked on my office door, which was open. He introduced himself and handed me his card. It described him as the Director of the World Gravity Preservation Society® or some such. [It's been 20 years, after all.] The card depicted him holding an earthworm that had to be 5 feet long and must have weighed several pounds. He said he thought his organization merited a story in the paper.

It was worth a shot. I interviewed him for about an hour and took notes long lost to the ravages of time. He played it straight, or as I suggested upslope, nuts.[302] His organization was purportedly determined to save giant earthworms from extinction because our planet's gravity entirely depends on them. "Once they went," he assured me, "we would all just float away."

In the end we didn't run the story. But for some reason that vignette popped into my noggin when I spied the cardinal.

Thinking back to that very real—if loony—business card this morning, I asked myself, how big *do* earthworms get?

But this story is off to a slow start. Let's give Dave a namesake named Dave. We can make our Dave bisexual, the same as an earthworm (and that's simply a biological fact with worms—I don't mean the comparison in any sort of pejorative sense). And we can loan him a cat as I so often do in these narratives. For today's purposes we'll offer up Sherlock.

Dave chefs at an upscale eatery downtown and lives in a garage apartment on the north side. He's a pro and his specialty is creation of desserts for which he utilizes dark chocolate which comes in squares that weigh about as much as a large earthworm.

---

302 As I've previously noted, my brother endured/enjoyed bipolar disorder and when he was manic he was extremely convincing regarding his varying versions of reality.

Dave is a seriously serial monogamist, so he's not constantly swinging back and forth. But his preferences drift between relationships so you never know whether he's going AC or DC next time around. *That's his business and none of ours.*

From Sherlock's standpoint Dave's principal virtue is possession of an opposable thumb (two actually, he's been quite careful with knives during his career). I've long observed that if cats had the same they'd be able to open cans on their own and wouldn't much need us.

Sherlock, by the way, is a jumper, somewhat like my dear old buddy Havoc who is pushing up a giant climbing rose these many years. He would leap from the floor to my shoulder so elegantly that he simply settled, barely availing himself of his claws. He'd also sail to the top of the refrigerator or a high bookshelf. He seemed so nearly weightless you would wonder, for just a sec, if the last of the giant earthworms had abruptly expired.

Sherlock's acrobatics tend to be more horizontal, flying across the bedroom to land on the comforter, bouncing to the sofa, then the countertop, then a leap to the floor and a bound to the table where cat meals occur locally. I don't have any high bookshelves these days and the fridge is beneath a cabinet so I don't suppose he'll face those tests of derring-do.

• Sherlock

"Mmmf!" exclaimed Dave as 7 pound Sherlock hurtled onto his stomach this morning, having launched across the sleeping quarters. "I hope you don't gain weight."

At the moment of impact Dave was reading the December, 2022, issue of *Harpers*® and had just come to the sentence: "Fifteen falcons, most of them headless, were found buried in a temple at Berenike along with a stele whose inscription reads IT IS IMPROPER TO BOIL A HEAD IN HERE."

That would make anyone think, but for a chef it suggests fairly profound philosophical questions. Like experts in any field the cooks of the world speak an insider lingo, a cryptolect if you will. For we outsiders the inscription seems pretty straight forward. Wherever the hell Berenike is, and whosoever's temple administrator commissioned the stele, someone expressed, in stone mind you, an opinion regarding the boiling of heads. We might wonder for a few minutes whether the opinion was formed after the birds' noggins were dissevered and cooked or if that decapitation and (perhaps?) stewing had been one of defiance by a subsequent tenant, if, in fact, there was any direct connection whatsoever between the interment of said fowl and the effort at proscription of said cookery. The presence of cooked heads was not mentioned in the quoted report.

But a serious chef, an initiate in the high art of culinary arcana, a utilizer of chocolate chunks approximately the weight of a large (now dead) earthworm, reads right through the immediate and peers into the mystery. Dave knows Berenike to have been an Egyptian city about 500 miles south of the modern Suez canal and in its heyday an important trading center on the Ancient Maritime Spice Route®. You see?

Back in the day the AMSR® was critical for cooks. Sans refrigeration flesh got a little "gamey" pretty fast and if you wanted return customers a healthy dose of cumin or coriander or turmeric could do the trick—as long as they didn't die of food poisoning first.

Also, Dave noted, the boiling was deemed "improper" but not specifically "prohibited." Wiggle room there.[303]

All the difference in the world.

He wondered if there are extant ancient Egyptian recipes for boiled heads? Dave recalls that when mummies were gift wrapped all of the organs were stashed in amphorae so as to be available to the owner in the afterlife. All of the organs *except the brain*,[304] which those high and far off folks believed had *no purpose*.[305] The skulls were simply drained. Did they eat them? And if so, with which exotic spices? Would they taste good with chocolate?[306]

At this point in the story Sherlock is curled and purring so we'll just let the two of them enjoy the rest of the day.

---

303 Appropriate in a story under the current title.
304 A true fact!
305 Another!
306 Then, one or two squares? Great chefs think outside the box.

Alone on a hill

    Your reaction to the above says worlds. How do you feel about that? What memories does it stir? Do you think the person or creature or object is feeling isolated or content? Can you describe the scene? Day or night? Overcast or sunny? Would you like to be there? Is there someone from your past you wish were placed in the situation you have just imagined?
    I think we've covered enough ground for your first therapy session, but I hope you'll think things over before next week when we'll take up the idea of "A loan on a hill."
    Melanie (remember Melanie?[307]) tells me that one of her most popular back-tats depicts a Buddha figure sitting cross-legged atop a mountain with a background of clouds and a few birds circling above. (Eagles? Vultures?) Her clients report that just knowing—to the extent that anyone can know anything, of course[308]—that the Buddha is sitting there between their shoulder blades calms them down.[309]
    As it happens, Melanie lives alone on a hill in a tiny modular home for the purchase of which she obtained a $45K loan (with $5K down) in 2010. [See? I wasn't simply playing with rhyme upslope.] It's a 20 year note with 6.47 percent interest which means if she stays put she'll end up paying something north of $200K (including property taxes, insurance and what the bank defines as "other expenses") for a unit that will likely have approximately no significant resale value. But her monthly out-of-pocket (all inclusive) is only $845+change which qualifies as affordable in these days of late-stage capitalism. So she's one of the lucky ones.
    Tattoos are not cheap, but I've observed that there are a whole raft of parlors these days downtown, in strip malls, beside hardware stores and taquerias and so forth. I've also noticed that

---

307 On page 145, not the professor we met on page 32. Why certain names recur here is anybody's guess.
308 See General Rule #10.
309 One might observe here that anyone who pays a ton of money to have things etched on their backsides where they will never see them clearly needs some calming. Xanax?

there are usually empty parking spaces adjacent to such establishments. That is not a sign of heavy commercial traffic so low rent housing is no small thing.

But what you want to know[310] is what she does in her time off, notwithstanding the fact that those of us who are self-employed don't actually have a lot of time off. Which mention reminds me of advice my Dear Old Dad gave me when I was around 20 years old. "Don't go into business for yourself. You'll never have time off."

He was and within six months I was as well. He was more or less right. I more or less solved the problem by: a) Remaining child-free; and b) Never incurring debt.[311] [Well, there was that one car. A mistake: "Fool me once."] Those two things I recommend without qualification. As Paul Simon® suggested, "A man gets tied up to the ground, he gives the world its saddest sound, its saddest sound."[312]

As it happens that song was released the year I turned 20, which might well have exerted some influence on my young self. I certainly took the "away, I'd rather sail away" to heart and spent much of the next 30 years in a camper, a canoe, in my hiking boots, or in a garden. I have to credit my early education: a mechanical drawing class in 8th grade, Home Repairs merit badge and learning the Pythagorean theorem at about that same time.

The 3:4:5 triangle is the starting place for most construction.

Perhaps unsurprisingly I became a builder.

I see I have wandered (well, obviously, given how I spent those many years) and you wanted to know about Melanie.

First off, one of the benefits of inking people is that you don't take your work home with you. So, other than bookkeeping, she has her evenings off, and she's pretty clear about Sundays.

Second, though she's got a mortgage (the "tied up to the ground" thing) she's avoided one of the greatest pitfalls widely available in this vail of tears. She does not now and never has owned a guinea pig. They stink to high heaven, as the saying goes.

---

310 See General Rule #10.
311 Reminding me of Ben Franklin, America's first polymath, whom until this very moment (9:00:24 EST, 10 January, 2023) I had credited with "Neither a borrower nor a lender be." But it's from Shakespeare.
Franklin's version is "Rather go to bed hungry than rise in debt." Works for me.
312 "El Condor Pasa," *Bridge over troubled water,* Columbia®, 1970

However, neither of those offer insight into what, exactly, she *does* with those precious off-hours. Let me think.

She *does* have a cat, the not-having of which is another common pitfall. [If you think this somehow throws my assertions regarding my peripatetic years into question, you should have seen Snook walk the gunnels of a canoe as we floated down a spring run in the Ocala National Forest®, trot ahead on a hike in the Alaskan boreal forest or curiously meander among Viking ruins in Newfoundland. Cats are great campers.]

Again, I have wandered.

Ah, I've got it! Melanie plays a bass ukulele! And sings!

If you ever heard her you'd surely agree that she puts a lot of effort into it. *A lot!* Also that it's fortunate for the other 7.9999 billion of us that she mostly keeps it to herself. Her day job may not pay all that well, but it is definitely one she ought not quit.

[Were it not for Mels opposable thumbs I suspect Moxie would leave. As it is he hides under the bed at the far end of the unit when she's playing and is greatly relieved when she takes the show outside in fair weather. The nearest neighbors less so, though they are a good way downhill.]

She has a bird feeder and goldfish in a bowl for which Moxie is grateful. A solo cat wants entertainment. Tail chasing has its limits.

Having disparaged her musical endeavors I think I ought to praise her other artistic effort. She composes haiku! A few of her clients have even asked her to ink it in! For instance Shelly has this one on her right thigh.

Softly hooting owl
In the autumn darkness
Is a friend a friend?

I think that's kind of nice. And this one on Gwen's right upper arm.

Ice on the limbs
A kiss in the afternoon
Alone on a hill.

Gosh, now we see Melanie as gifted! A poet with a pointy inky pen! I wonder what she'll come up with next?

Rustication

Now we're talking! It doesn't get any better than this!

Remember Norm Clayton? Back on page 99? Ordering *machaca* and drinking high-end scotch? That Norm?

Well, some of us do, poor fellow. That was his last supper.

So I guess he won't join us in this little adventure.[313]

Let's see. How about Jeremy Bonners? He was at that dinner too and, as luck would have it, *didn't die the next day*. Whew! He and we are in luck.

Jeremy sells mattresses at one of those outlet shops with the endless special "sales" and a blow-up figure at curbside, flapping in the breeze. He'll assure you that the particular model you're considering is "hotel quality" and that the current price is $400 or $600 below list. He'll lay out a thin cloth cover and a similarly draped pillow and encourage you to lie down. ["Fall asleep if you like."] He'll offer free delivery too.

[But ask him about alien life forms and he'll button up in a heartbeat. I think he knows more than he's willing to let on.]

It must be a lonely business as those parking lots seem even emptier than the ones adjacent to tattoo joints.[314]

Well, last Saturday Tanya Michelson was shopping for a new bed. When she stopped into Mr. Mattress® Jeremy jolted to alertness as he had just about dozed off in his slightly reclining office chair. [Friday had been a late night, out carousing with Redge.]

He nodded at his prospective victim and let her wander around between the several dozen floor models. He'd learned not to hurry a customer.

When she seemed to settle between two mid-range units— one $1199 (REDUCED TO $699!) and another $1399 (REDUCED TO $749!) he stood and approached her.

"Good morning! I see you're looking at our best-selling

---

313 For those of you keeping score at home, note that this is the second character I've snuffed in these pages. Kurt Vonnegut would be proud of me. (See page 44.) Pete doesn't count, he died six books ago.

314 See page 151 if you've been skipping around in here. You *do realize* that these stories are meant to be read in order, do you not?

hotel quality mattresses."

"Oh, they are?"

"Indeed they are. You've seen we have others that are quite a bit more expensive, but hotel operators know what they need. Good quality, very comfortable and durable, but sensibly priced."

Tanya was pressing her hand on each one in turn. "They seem firm enough."

"Would you like to try them out?"

"I guess."

Jeremy fetched a coverlet and a pillow. "Which one first?"

"I guess this." She gestured toward the cheaper of the two.

He placed the pillow and carefully spread the cover. "There you go."

Tanya set her purse aside and lay down. "Nice." Then started to get up.

"Why don't you try it out for a bit? Get a sense of how it would work at home. Are you a back sleeper or side?"

"Side."

"Well take your time. Roll around. Do you sleep well? Generally, I mean."

"I haven't been, but I may have solved that this morning."

"Oh, this mattress?" [He grew hopeful.]

"No. I read an article on cosmology that answered the question that's been keeping me awake nights."

Jeremy frowned. This wasn't going to work with his usual spiel about how an old mattress was often the problem. But he knew that the best way to engage a customer was often a question.

"What was that?"

"I couldn't understand how everything came from nothing."

"That *is* a tough one." He decided to take a chance, this being the South and all. "Isn't the traditional answer God?"

"Yeah. You hear that. But it didn't make sense."

"How?"

"Then where did God come from?"

"I see. So what do you think now?"

"It's really pretty simple. When the singularity went bang it split into matter and antimatter, with the amounts equal, so it's still a net nothing. It's just divided in half."

"But what made it split in half?"

"Nothing." Then, "I just know I'll sleep better tonight. But thanks for the demo and I'll think about a purchase."

Now, "nothing" might not seem like much, but that conversation got Jeremy to thinking about the ins and outs of everything. His mental framework took on the aspect of a rusticated stone wall, with ideas piled together and deep grooves between them. Who he was, where he was going, how he was doing, what was his future? How high is up? [That's always a good one.]

He recalled something Norm Clayton had said during his last supper: "Sometimes you have to change your thinking. Like the fellow who decided to go to the moon and climbed a tree. It was all going pretty well ... at first."

This thing about nothing was a game changer. If, ultimately, it all adds up to nothing why was he sitting in a Mr. Mattress® store six days a week? Why wasn't he trying for the moon? Maybe not climbing, but, at least, shooting for?

After closing that night Jeremy stretched out on the mattress Tanya had vacated in the morning, thinking that he might find inspiration there. "Nothing," he said aloud. "Nothing."

It was, in fact, comfortable. [Most new mattresses are. It's age that tells the tale.] He fell asleep, perchance to dream.

Dream he did. A doozy. He was on a beach, shell shopping in the strand, and Tanya was there. With him![315] In a bikini! It seemed they walked for miles while the surf lapped. She was telling him something but he couldn't quite make it out.

They came upon a boat washed up against the shore, rocking in the waves. His companion climbed in and gestured for him to do the same. He shoved it off before scrambling over the stern. "Angel," he said.

"Who, me?"

"No the boat."

"What?"

"On the stern. The name.[316]"

Tanya turned a key and the motor coughed and started. In 20 minutes land was out of sight and she switched it off and jumped overboard. When she bobbed up her hair was wreathed with seaweed. In the clear water he could see her legs had become a tail. A mermaid! "Nothing," she whispered and blew him a kiss before swimming away.

Hours seemed to pass before he tried to restart the engine.
Nothing. He was gripped with fear and woke, wide eyed.
Nothing.

---

315 Likely due to smelling a trace of her shampoo scent on the pillow.
316 Yes, Pete's boat. (See page 80.) This saves me the trouble of inventing a new craft, and Pete obviously doesn't need it.

How high is up?

We asked this question on the previous page, but didn't take time to consider it. This is something like the question "Is that in walking distance?"

We "know" what a person "means" when asking, but it's pretty open ended. After all, the first human residents of North America apparently walked here from Asia and their ancestors walked to Siberia from Africa. Then they walked to Tierra del Fuego and Labrador. This means that an accurate answer—unless the location is on an island—is always "yes."

Miami? *"Si."* Havana? *"No."* Antarctica? *"Nada.*[317]*"*

[Of course, if we're only talking about "distance" as versus feasibility everywhere on the planet is so located.]

Our titular question is more difficult, seeing as it doesn't come down to yes or no. Further confusion ensues when one considers Einstein's theories[318] and all that flowed therefrom. Illustrations seem to depict gravity as something more like a depression in a trampoline due to the curvature of space-time. Objects will roll toward wherever you're standing and the dip moves as you walk around, uphill becoming downhill, step by step.

Sherry Ratner, the birthday girl we met on page 100, had an amusing take on the question when she was 19. She and her boyfriend had snuck into a neighbor's back yard and were fooling around on a trampoline after smoking some pretty potent weed. He asked ... "How high ... yes or no?"

She answered "Yes, I mean," Giggle ... "No?" They collapsed on the bouncy surface laughing like hyenas. [Maybe you had to be there.]

Sherry's all grown up now and as previously noted is selling cars. She's no less honest than most of her ilk and as we've also noted somewhere upslope few of us can pretend to complete frankness. Lies just seem so easy most of the time, about little things of course. It's the whoppers that tarnish one's reputation,

---

317 Practicing the old *español* we are!
318 To my knowledge Uncle Albert didn't know about the giant earthworms discussed on page 147.

though small ones can sometimes niggle.

In Sherry's case the usual spin about used vehicles has become second nature and, really, that's more polish than out and out prevarication. She's never knowingly sold anyone a serious lemon. It's more along the lines of "I put a customer in one of these last year and she came by the other day to tell me how glad she was," when that never actually happened. Or, "140,000 is pretty low mileage for a ten year old Honda®," which is not a fact, but a matter of opinion designed to instill buyer confidence. Or, "We're only making a couple hundred at this price." (As if.)

But we're thinking "up" in this disquisition so let's go on a hike with Sherry and her bouncy boyfriend Bob back in their early 20s. They were in the Canadian Rockies® not too many air miles from the cabin where four attorneys holed up after a plane crash in a tale of almost magical transformation[319] back in 1999. The hike was during a camping excursion shortly after their graduation.

They had walked way up a mountain with heavy backpacks and set up camp in a meadow beside a pristine stream. A helpful outfitter had told them where and how and even assured them that the water was potable. It was as described and they were gloriously alone in a breathtakingly beautiful setting with snow-capped peaks in the near and far distance, surrounded by an evergreen forest, camped amid tufts of alpine flowers.

"Is that in reasonable[320] walking distance?" Bob had queried.

He assured them it was. Fortunately the helpful advisor also reminded them to hang their food "all of it" in a tree at night and to sling it a good distance from their campsite. "There *are* grizzlies up there at this time of year.[321]"

Sherry had also read footnote #111 and told Bob, "You can go first." He didn't say anything at the time but neither did he forget. I imagine it was part of the mental case he put together when break-up time rolled around somewhat later.

But enough about that. They spent a fine week on that mountain and we might assume they frolicked[322] a bit in the altogether. [We don't know for sure since they were inside a tent.]

---

319 "In which four Norsemen consume antique rice," *Can we have archaic and idiot-2,* BUB, 1999, 2009
320 We see here how a modifier gives the query a bit of clarity.
321 He added the advice we read in footnote #111.
322 Haven't had a hot'n'steamy for a while.

One crystalline night they took their sleeping pads out of the shelter and lay down staring at the stars so dramatically visible in the absence of urban illumination.

"Amazing!" she whispered,[323] awestruck.

"Yeah!" he retorted, almost under his breath.

"To think that all this came from nothing." *Sottovoce*[324] this time.

"Whaddya mean?"

"Big bang."

"That's just a theory."

"But it's the best explanation that comports with observational astronomy."

"I think it's stupid."

"What's your version?"

"God."

Tanya didn't reply but neither did she forget. It became part of the mental case she put together when break-up time rolled around not long after the expedition.

In response to her silence Bob spoke up again. "I suppose you think life on earth started on its own too. God is a better explanation" [That clinched it. Hoo boy!]

"Does that bother you?" he insisted.

"No," she lied, quietly. [A little white one that would niggle for years.]

Tanya thought back to that time just yesterday[325] when she read that all of the bases of DNA and RNA have been discovered in meteorites: Adenine, guanine, uracil, cytosine, thymine plus ribose, a sugar necessary for life. Life bombs whirring around the universe. Boggling.

Life happens, she thought, and it all comes up or down to nothing.

---

323 I realize a whisper doesn't seem to warrant an exclamation point but it was a *forceful* whisper.
324 *Italiano!*
325 Mid-January, 2023

Purr

Sherlock, lying on my chest just now, suggested the title for this one, but I could be purring too. One and a half cups of Joe and about 40 pages from the escape hatch, what's not to like?

This is way different than, say, being an astronaut or cosmonaut on the International Space Station® in recent months. Here I am, comfortably lying on a mattress (or alien life form, as the case may be) with a safe exit just downslope. They've been floating around up there with a disabled escape vessel until this week when the Russians sent up a replacement. That had to be a little unsettling.

As Vonnegut asked, "If this isn't nice, what is?"[326]

An escape hatch, or vessel for that matter, is a lot like a pre-nup. Just knowing there's an easy out is calming—much more so, I would wager, than having a back-tat of Buddha meditating.

Of course most pre-nups are created by lawyers for rich and famous folks who plan to marry someone less so, in order to protect their riches and fame from the other in the event of a split.

Doesn't that just shout "true love!"?

It can also have the collateral effect of ensuring fidelity on pain of losing access to the goodies. (Am thinking Melania just now.)

But not everyone and not always.

Remember Bertie and Tara? Y'know, feeding ducks in France back on page 46? Well they returned from that vacay more in love than when they left. They married not long afterward. They'd come back feeling more egalitarian as well, after their exposure to a culture with free education, free healthcare, earlier retirement, pensions, powerful unions and all the rest. How could they not? How could they not?

So when they decided to wed they asked a friend, Delbert Hunter,[327] to create a pre-nup that would guarantee an absolutely even split of *everything* (excepting individual pets or children, of

---

[326] *If this isn't nice, what is? Advice for the young,* Seven Stories Press®, 2013

[327] A lawyer we last met in "Sweet Surrender," in *Cede Catalog-giving it all away,* BUB, 2021

course) in the event of divorce. They felt that, young as they were, there was no telling if one or the other might generate more income over the years, and being freshly egalitarianized they wanted to swear to each other that hers and his were "ours," no matter what. No matter what.

If there is a downside to such a warm and generous contract it would be that it cedes leverage in the event of possible philandering. You only want to make that sort of agreement with someone you *entirely* trust. Or, one supposes, in what is known as an "open marriage."

My view, from experience, is that such an "open" arrangement is fraught. On the other I can also attest from experience that being unmarried and unopen with mingled assets and no contract other than what might be called a "handshake agreement" is at least as bad.

Interpersonal relationships are ever thus because they involve other human beings. Ooooh. We've found another GR!

General Rule #12: "Interpersonal relationships are fraught because they involve other human beings."

I'm happy to report that Bertie and Tara enjoyed several very happy years and then some reasonably happy years and next some slightly difficult years. Then Tara had an affair. Worse, it wasn't a one'n'done. She fell for another man who gave her that "dizzy dancing way you feel when every fairy tale comes real."[328]

But I'll give it to her, she was straight up with Bertie who was well aware they had been drifting, separate vacations and so forth. "Honey," she said, using the noun she had applied to him for nearly ever, "Mitchell gives me a dizzy dancing feeling."

"You mean the waiter we met at that Mexican joint?"

She nodded. "I guess I want a divorce."

Bertie put on a stoic face though we can guess he was all torn up inside. Sure, the bloom was off the rose, but there had to be some ego in there. Losing out to a waiter? And a *bad* waiter at that? (He didn't know that Tara had eaten at La Bamba® with a girlfriend one time when Mitch was in the *good* slot. Charmed her pants off, he did.)

What they didn't see coming was the fight over the cat.

Big Mama had been with them for 8 years at that point and was equally dear to them both—with a purr like a motor boat.

Custody battle.

Time to lawyer up. (Sigh.)

---

328 Joni Mitchell®, "Clouds," *Clouds,* Reprise®, 1969

Robovac

    Honestly, I had absolutely no idea how dirty my house was before I purchased a robotic vacuum cleaner. That isn't what this story is about, but I thought this deserved full disclosure. In self defense I would guess that most people share such ignorance since the interior of a regular vacuum bag is not generally subject to close examination. Maybe if you own one of those tube types, with a transparent body you know what I've seen.
    But here's a thing. Unless you get one of those really high tech robots that self-empties, you have to remove the dust bin and dump it pretty frequently. Well, well. I was so amazed at the quantity of detritus at first that I began to empty it into a waste basket in my bathroom and just let it build up, to get a longer sample so to speak. How long would it take to fill the thing?
    Before long I began to have tiny fleas[329] jumping on me when I was—hmm, want to be delicate here—oh, I've got it—seated.
    After about a week I realized that my unit was picking up flea eggs and they were hatching in the trash, a problem easily solved, but also reassuring. This Eufy®[330] really sucks!
    Some of the denizens of the old cat ranch were afraid of it, one ignored it, but calico Clare [RIP] was the queen. When the robot was scooting around, bouncing off the walls and furniture, she would sit mid floor and let it carom off her, sometimes taking a swipe with her paw.
    This reminds me of something clever I read yesterday.
    Cat: Has claws at the end of its paws.
    Comma: Has pause at the end of its clause.
    Okay, so I'm easily amused. In any event for the purposes of this excursion I'm going to loan Clare and the Eufy® to Olivia Turnbull who we met on page 36, shin-deep in warm mud. We recall that by the end of that gripping story we knew her well enough to label her with the hypocoristic, "Liv," and when we last mentioned her she was getting naked with an unnamed

---

329 How indoor cats get fleas is a numinous mystery.
330 We last met a Eufy® in "Magic Carpet Ride," *Fifty wheys to love your liver,* BUB, 2018 [Wow. I've had mine for almost 5 years!]

companion.[331]

Now she has a cat [Clare for those of you with short memories] and a vacuum, and, let's see, oh, right, a significant other! [The previous hot'n'steamy preceded cohabitation by a few months.]

So now Liv *and* Addissae have a cat, a vac, etc.

Addissae is also a post-doc at the university, though she is in the physics department, not the chem lab. She came here by way of Happy Appy.[332]

The first thing you'd probably notice about Adsie is her height, and you wouldn't be surprised to learn that she went to Appy on a basketball scholarship. It was during hours and hours and hours of shooting baskets in high school that she began to think in terms of infinitesimals regarding the arc of thrown rubber objects, obviously leading to planets, gravity and the space-time continuum.

You'd probably also notice her red hair, though these days hair color, particularly among the young, is variable. I mean, she *had* red hair when I last saw her but it could well be turquoise or lime green today. Let me check.

...

OMG! She shaved her head! Her noggin is somewhat earth-shaped—an oblate spheroid turned on its side. Nose: Everest.

Correction: Liv shaved Adsie's head.

It was just the Saturday before last that Adsie said, "Sugarpie, I think I want to shave my head."

**Her partner's initial reaction was "!" accompanied by an eye-roll. "You sure?"

"Ever since I read footnote #121 I've been thinking about doing it. It made me curious."

"Whatever. I guess you can always grow it back."

"Will you still love me?"

"Stupid question dear one. I think you'd better let me help though. I don't want to see you all cut up."

So Liv went at it. First with scissors, collecting the long lime green locks and setting them aside, then snapping some pics of the crewcut with her cell.

Next she tucked a towel around her lover's neck and soaped her head with Dr. Bronner's®.

---

331 Hot'n'*steamy* for darn sure. Recall they were showering together on page 37.
332 Appalachian State University® up in Boone, N. Car.

"Oh that feels good!" Which encouraged the barber half of the duo to prolong the soaping as sort of a cranial massage.

Next the razor, handled with care. The whole operation took the better part of an hour, ending with Adsie jumping into the shower to rinse off soap and residual fur.

She called out, "You wouldn't believe how this feels! The spray on my head! Incredible!"

Over the course of last week Adsie kept up with the exclamations. "The breeze! The sun on my scalp! The heat from overhead lighting! The pillow! My hat!" Then, "Liv, I'm really <u>feeling</u> my head for the first time! Really, really!"

Well, it didn't take long. Just one week. Last Saturday Liv announced, "My turn." [Rather than waste valuable pixels I'll let you return to the ** on page 162 and switch names.]

So we have two oblate spheroids making one think of the well known two-body problem in classical mechanics in which it is assumed that the pair only interact with one another, that the only force acting on the one comes from the other and that all other bodies are ignored.

Of course that's the *theory,* and for the most part that's true of our pair of lovers, though the naked head thing might be pushing some sort of limit. You see, others often want to *touch* a newly bald head previously hidden below lime green, red, turquoise, brown, blond, auburn, brunette or black hair. [This is not dissimilar to what is often reported by Black people regarding the touching of kinky hair by whites. Generally children.]

Yesterday, the first time Liv arrived at the lab bald, Oscar ran his hand over her head. "Nice," he observed. "Very nice."

"Watch it Bosco[333]!"

"Couldn't help myself. You're practically an oblate spheroid now! And a shiny one at that!"

"Thanks, but remember it's for looking, not touching."

"OK, I get it." He slouched off to his lab table.

Adsie on the other hand had a somewhat different experience in the physics department. There it was Phyllis who took liberties. She first commented, "New look baby!" Then asked, "Can I touch?"

General Rule #13: "Ask first."

"Sure. I'm getting a kick out of experiencing the nerves in my scalp in new and interesting ways." She tilted her head since

---

[333] His work nickname. She's a little sharp with him because he's inclined to hit on her despite knowing her gender orientation.

Phyllis is almost a foot shorter than our former ball player.

Her fellow post-doc delicately stroked the proffered surface, her long nails very slightly dragging on the naked skin.

"Damn girl, that is sexy as hell. You're sending shivers all the way to my distal digits." She bent further. "Don't stop!"

Phyllis continued the gentle strokes then leaned in and kissed the crown with just a hint of tongue.

"Yikes!"

What was happening reminds us of the two-body problem in general relativity, where the one with the larger mass attracts the one with the smaller in ways that can't be precisely calculated.

If Adsie were to act on her immediate impulse, reacting to this frankly sexualized interaction, she might well invite Phyllis over to play, likely creating a three-body problem[334], assuming Liv is open to the idea. [There is no closed-form solution for such a situation because the resulting dynamical system is chaotic for most initial conditions. With a Ph.D. in higher math and theoretical physics Addissae Turner is well aware of the potential for chaos and resolved to talk it over with her amour first.]

That evening, waiting for Liv to come home she was watching the Eufy® carom around the room and found herself wondering about the vacuum's software, trying to figure out if its actions were random or programmed and "What if there were two?" Three?

Clare was sitting atop the thing, evidently enjoying the ride.

When Liv arrived and after an embrace and a kiss Adsie said, "Phyllis asked to touch my head today."

"Bosco didn't ask, he just went for it. The jerk."

"I let her. It was pretty amazing. Let me show you."

"Okay. Sure."

The physicist duplicated the action described at the top of this page and her partner had a similar reaction. In short order one thing led to another.[335]

Later, fixing supper, Adsie came up behind Liv and stroked her noggin again.

"Mmmm. Anytime, sugar."

"Honey, can you imagine what that would feel like with four hands?"

"You mean mine?"

"Not exactly."

---

334 In classical mechanics.
335 You got it. Hot'n'steamy.

Extremities ...

He was spread-eagled. Limbs stretched and staked. A column of ants was marching over his half-naked torso. The sun. Oh the sun! A chain saw revved and he looked to see a tree that would surely fall in his direction. "My god!" he said, or thought, or thought he said. "I'm wearing the wrong T-shirt!" [Ditto.]

"Where am I? Why is this happening? I'm going to die!" A pause[336], then, "I'm wearing the wrong tee! V-neck not crew!"

Richard woke with a shudder and reached to turn on the bedside lamp. Chomsky stood and stretched and walked across the bed, purring. Our troubled nightmare victim stroked his companion and asked aloud, "Where did that one come from?"

Cats know but seldom answer.

"Must have been those hot dogs with kraut just before I cashed in." [That's right. Blame the food.]

Chomsky nodded but said nothing and rolled on his back to suggest a tummy rub.

I'm thinking it's more likely pressure at work that's been triggering Richard's fearsome dreams. This has been going on a few nights a week for a month or more and if he keeps blaming his meals he'll probably develop some kind of eating disorder.

Workplace stress affects a lot of us, often in unpredictable ways. Some eat or drink to excess, run up credit card balances, post cat pictures to Instagram®, or play pickle ball. Symptoms can include heightened blood pressure and frequent colds.[337]

Richard's work keeps him on edge all the time, performing repetitive tasks that require absolute accuracy for as much as four hours at a time with only one 15 minute break.

He tries very hard but too often falls short of his personal targets. He wants to be the very best but sometimes—no not sometimes—*frequently* experiences self doubt. Couldn't he do better? Of course he could. Then why not?

Now we catch up with him at Walmart® as he pulls a shopping cart from the stand and places it in front of the next customer. That went well enough. And again. And again.

---

336 At the end of a clause!
337 Study released just this week—late January—viruses love stress.

But what?

We didn't learn much about Jill Steenbergen back on page 43—other than that she is a patient and dedicated Montessori teacher—so I thought we should pick up on her story here. [By the way, Jasper, having the relatively short attention span of a normal 5-year-old, forgot about his plan to cut the captive worm in half. Jill returned the lowly critter to the wild at the end of the school year.]

Jill is pretty darn serene unlike the fellow we met on the previous page who is—not to put too fine a point on it—a bundle of nerves. She has a record player! And LPs! Classical! She dances! She glides across her living room languidly gesturing in much the manner of a conductor leading a waltz.

On fair weekends you could catch up with her *en plein air*[338], standing beside an easel, brush and palette in hand, laying on the oil paint in an impressionist depiction of the montane landscape. Ah! Yes! Rather *oui!* She hums! *Chopin* I think.

But what we want to know is what she *thinks*, not what she does. After all, interiority is the interesting part of pretty much all of us. Right?

Let's see. Ah, I've got it. This morning she's ruminating about a conversation she had a week ago with Andrea who was telling her about an episode of some TV show where the lead character was in a serious pickle, as well as its upshot. Andrea said the man was named Stan. [This a.m. she's also thinking about last night.]

"Stan would be a perfect match for you."

"But Andrea, he's an actor."

"I mean a man like Stan."

"I'll bite. Why?"

"He's just so funny!"

"What makes you think I need funny in my life?"

"You're ..." here Andrea paused ... "You seem kind of serious most of the time. Too serious."

"What?"

---

338 It's been a while since we had our selves some *française*. [Using the feminine case here since we're talking about Jill.]

"I mean, you know, like painting. It's so goal-directed. Like your teaching, you're so all about that. And your violin lessons. And your French lessons. And the crosswords. Do you ever just have fun? Oh, and the music. "

"What's wrong with my music?"

"Classical? Don't you ever want to boogey?"

"I'm good. I'm serene. See page 166. And I get things done."

"Do you ever *not?* Anyway girl, I have a friend who's a lot like Stan and I want the two of you to meet. I'm gonna set you up."

"What if I don't *want* to be set up?"

"Give it a chance. OK? For me? Here's his number and I'll give him yours."

So Jill had agreed, Andie being her bestie and all. To meet. That's all. To meet. She's so not certain that she wanted this. She could spend any evening reading and spare herself the dressing up and the drive. As it happens the meeting was set for last night which is why she's thinking the following things this morning[339] as she paints.

Stan[340] had turned out to be funny in a low key way—not "har, har," but more a gentle half-guffaw—and seemed to be kind. He also smelled OK.[341] They'd met at a quiet restaurant and had an extended conversation during a leisurely meal. When time came for the check she'd insisted on splitting. No sense in incurring an obligation this early in a relationship.

Bingo! General Rule #14: "Don't incur obligations at the start of a possible romance."

But she has to admit that what he'd said about geocaching intrigued her. He'd said "I geocache most weekends, in fair weather."

Like most among us Jill had never heard the word before and asked. "Geo-what?" [I didn't have a clue myself before Stan explained in the next several sentences.]

"It's sort of a treasure hunt."

"Treasure, like buried treasure?"

"Not buried. Never buried. But people hide stuff."

"O ... K?"

"Then you try to find it. Using a smart phone."

---

339 21 January, 2023. Since it's pretty chilly she's painting in her studio with *Chopin* on the turntable.
340 No need to come up with a new name.
341 Important in my view. Kind of a quick quality eval.

"How does that work?"

"You use a free app called Geocaching®. That gives you a map with thousands of hidden caches. Then using your GPS gets you within about 30 feet of the target and you have to search. What you look for is something out of place. Like being a detective."

"But what[342] do you find?"

"You never know until you find it. Could be big, could be tiny. One time I found a tackle box under a bush, another time one of those aluminum tubes that hold high end cigars, there was a peanut butter jar once and a shoebox. All kinds of things."

"And then?"

"At minimum there's a piece of paper inside with the names of everyone who's found it and you add your own, while also posting your name on the app page associated with the cache. Sometimes, in the bigger ones, there are collections of odds and ends and you can take one or leave one. A troll doll, a Cracker Jack® prize, a penny ... could be anything."

The whole idea somewhat excited our protagonist as she turned it over this morning. This man was quite possibly *even more* goal directed than she. And yet it was so abstract, so directed at what seemed to be an entirely meaningless end. Kind of Zen®, really.

But what was it he'd said about muggles? Isn't that from Harry Potter®? Oh, right, when the cache is in a public place he said you have to make sure no muggles see you claiming the prize, because muggles might steal the cache after you put it back. Or phone the police if they think your actions are suspicious. Or the bomb squad for heaven's sake.

Jill is serene enough to be pretty darn self-assured and late this morning she phoned Stan and asked if she might go geocaching with him sometime.

"How about next Saturday, if the weather suits?"

"Sounds good, Stan. Sounds like fun."[343]

When she told Andrea about the plan her friend was thrilled. "Oh girl! You're gonna have fun![344]"

---

342 Note the is the third time our title has appeared in the body of the text.
343 Fun? Is Jill loosening up? Stay tuned!
344 Yes! She is! Probably.

Geocaching®

Gotta say, Stan was thrilled[345] at the idea of partnering in his pursuit of what essentially amounts to a concept. The open-endedness was the great draw, but having someone to share it with added a sort of concreteness. "We" found a "thing," instead of "I" found an "idea." He'd have a witness! A co-conspirator!

So Saturday morning when he picked up Jill he was filled with generosity. He showed her the Geocaching® map on his phone and told her to go ahead and pick any dot within a reasonable[346] driving distance. She tapped on a site near Weaverville.

"Ah," he said, expanding the map view, "Looks like the Vance birthplace."

"Vance?[347]"

"Zebulon Vance, the first governor of North Carolina from the west, and a staunch defender of slavery as well as slave owner."

"You sure we want to go there?"

"Ah Jill, that's long ago and finding a cache there isn't like honoring that old bastard. Main thing is it's a public space so geocaching is OK."

"But are we somehow honoring him?"

"Don't think so. Y'know just last year the City of Asheville dismantled its Vance Monument, part of the general dismantling of Confederate stuff around the south."

"Oh, right. Saw something about that. But I never get downtown. Didn't know it was already gone."

"And who knows? The geocache might entail a direct repudiation. The people doing geocaches might not be the same crowd as the Sons of the Confederacy® members who defend the old South and insist on its glory."

"I guess."

"And recall that the SOC® tried to prevent Bothwell, our author, from being sworn into office back in 2009. If they'd

---

345 Perhaps more than Andrea. See last graf on page 168.
346 Same modifier as per walking on page 157.
347 She is evidently new to these parts.

succeeded his life could have taken some different track. You and I might never have existed! He might have moved to Canada!"

"Yikes!"

The edifying chit-chat continued as they proceeded north some 15 minutes from Asheville, whence they entered the state historic site. Though no check-in is required, Stan stopped in at the visitor center to explain their goal and assure the authorities that their presence was totally hobbyist. It took a while and Jill passed the time texting with Andie.

```
YOU'RE ON A DATE!
I GUESS.
YOU'RE HAVING FUN!
I GUESS.
ETC.
I GUESS.
ETC.
I GUESS.[348]
```

When Stan finally returned he said the docent had wanted a complete explanation since the initial "We're just looking" had been deemed inadequate if not weird and possibly illegal.

While the GPS had brought them to the Birthplace it was hard to pin down. Being within about 30 feet of the goal put them more or less near several of the seven buildings, including the slave quarters.

"That is where the Vances lived," Stan indicated. "And this is where up to 25 slaves lived." He gestured toward a rough cabin.

"And Vance is a North Carolina hero?".

"Among some. He was a huge advocate for slavery, so his heroism is an acquired taste."

"No thanks."

"Got you there."

Now our Sherlock Holmesian couple have begun to zero in on their goal. What, here—among reconstructed slavery-era log cabins—might be "out of place?"

There is the usual tourist trash: Kleenex, beverage bottles, cig butts. There is the tourist info residue: Pamphlets, maps, more pamphlets. But what's this?

This!

A plastic sippy cup artfully lodged behind a park bench!

Carefull now, are there any muggles around?

No. So proceed.

---

348 Tip for future writers. This sort of intimacy is what makes your characters more "real."

"Go ahead, Jill. You can open it."

She pulled the plastic container from its resting place and pried off the lid to reveal some slightly moldy juice remnants.

Hmm. On they go.

What's that? Behind a post under that porch? A BandAid® box. One of those old tin ones from back before everything went cardboard! Stan gestured a kind of "*voila.*"

Muggles about? No. [Not a hugely popular "tourist attraction."]

Jill pulled the container from its covert location and turned it in hand.

"Go ahead," Stan urged.

She snapped it open. Antique BandAids®.

Jill was beginning to think this whole effort was a little bit boring and a lot stupid when she spied a Brown Cow® yogurt container wedged next to a foundation stone back where the porch attached to the slave cabin. She crawled on her stomach to reach the thing and brushed dirt off her sweatshirt and jeans after the recovery. "Your turn," she said, handing over her find. "My luck doesn't seem good today."

"But you found *this.*"

"We'll see."

Stan removed the plastic cover. "Wow!" He plucked out a folded paper bearing a dozen names of previous finders. "This is it!" He handed the list to Jill. "You can add ours!"

While she inked their IDs he extracted another page, this one typed.

CONGRATULATIONS GEOCACHER! GOOD WORK! BUT NOW CONSIDER THIS. BETWEEN 17 AND 25 ENSLAVED PEOPLE LIVED IN THIS BUILDING, SOME BOUGHT AND SOLD FOR AS LITTLE AS $1. ONLY FIVE NAMES SURVIVE AND ONLY ONE WITH A <u>LAST</u> NAME. LEAH ERWIN, A COOK. THERE WERE RICHARD AND AGGIE, MARRIED; JIM, THE BLACKSMITH; AND VENUS, THE NANNY. IN 1860, 50% OF BUNCOMBE COUNTY'S DENIZENS WERE ENSLAVED. FIFTY. FIFTY. FIFTY.

"Oh," Jill whispered. "Oh."

They returned the papers to the container and Jill made the return crawl. The drive back south was a quiet one.

When Stan dropped her off at home he asked, "Next Saturday?"

"I'll have to think about it." [Don't we all?]

Don't we all?

Early squirrels and late

Get the bird seed. Hmm. I think that's another GR.

General Rule #15: "Early squirrels get the bird seed."

Honestly, too much emphasis is generally applied per birds and worms. When I spread a fruit'n'nut mix on my deck railing each morning the squirrels are there *way* ahead of the birds.

That's something Stan has noticed as well. He does the same on his deck.[349]

So we have now learned that Stan is a suburban animal lover and isn't that nice? It's one thing to go chasing abstractions on weekends, but quite another to be a steady source of nutrition for birds and small mammals. He's not the sort, like a former neighbor of mine, to refer to members of the subfamily *sciurinae* as "rats with bushy tails." They are our furry friends.

Stan paints houses and occasionally works with Patsy who we met on page 62. She's better with ladders, completely cool 25 feet up under a soffit. He's happier in the 10 foot range. Having a death grip on an aluminum rung and sweating like the dickens is not conducive to experiencing a fully pleasant day at work. [Acrophobia for sure.] As we've previously noted, there's really nothing quite as pleasant as being pleasant[350].

But otherwise he's right up there in Patsy's class. No holidays! No holidays!

Working together they've, of course, exchanged life stories as workers will. You already read about the biggest "thing" in Patsy's life—her divorce from the ice cream man. [If it evades you you can go back to page 64.] But what of Stan?

Well, well. He has heretofore avoided the trauma of marital break-up by not going marital. A few close calls, yes. But nothing institutionally aimed at theoretical permanence, or theoretically aimed at the institution. Nor has he been irresponsible—vasectomy in his 20s and quite careful regarding transmissible bacteria. But he very nearly participated in a kind of brilliant, kind of crazy armed robbery. (!)(!)

---

349 Which, frankly, warms this author's heart.

350 A concept which has recurred multiple times in this masterpiece since its first mention on page 14.

He admits he was lucky. He was, then, young and stupid. On the other hand, perhaps overly but luckily cautious.

"I mean, the other three apparently made out like bandits, which they were, and haven't been heard from since," as he told his fellow worker.

You see, one night, back when Stan was about 23, the four of them were sitting around on Aubrey's porch, passing a joint and generally feeling mellow. Aubrey abruptly turned serious.

"Do you know how much cash the mouse factory collects daily?"[351]

"You mean Disney World®, man?" Herman queried.

"Damn straight I do."

"So, how much, man?" This from Ken.

"Millions. In cash. Every damn day."

"So what, ma-an?" [Either of the above.]

"You know how all those characters, the ones in costume? You know, how they pop up?"

"What? Pop up?"

"The Mickeys and Minnies and Donalds and Goofies and all. They just pop up."

"Okay."

"There's tunnels. All under."

"So?"

"That's where the fruit loops in drag pop up from."

"And?"

"That's where they drop the cash."

"What? Drop?"

"From all the concessions. The cash is dropped in the tunnel and collected in an office near the airfield."

"That's crazy talk."

"No. My buddy Garr works there. He's told me how every day the cash goes to that office and every night at 6 p.m., sharp, a Brinks® truck pulls in to haul it to a bank."

"So?"

"It's next to the airfield."

"They got an airfield?"

"Private. You think the bigwigs fly commercial?"

"So what?"

Aubrey sighed. "I'm a pilot."

"And?"

"I can rent a plane."

---

351 This was back in the 70s when less business was conducted via plastic.

"And?"
"We fly in just before 6, on a weekend."
"Why a weekend?"
"Bigger take."
"Then?"
"We disarm the Brinks® guys, grab the money and fly."
"Where to?"
"An abandoned road on a cattle ranch northeast of here."
"And?"
"We climb into my SUV and drive away."
"I dunno man."
"You think that'll work?"
"Sounds too easy."
"Who's in?"
"Me."
"Me."
"Stan?"
"Gotta think on it."

As he told Patsy, he felt he had to agree to join in, given that he'd been party to the planning, but when time came for take-off he'd stayed away. He's certain the others had proceeded. "Evening robbery. Late squirrels collecting their nuts I guess."

"Was it in the news?" she'd asked.

"No. But my take is that Disney® wouldn't have wanted to report it. No use letting others know how easy it had been. The thing is, Aubrey and Herman and Ken? They disappeared. I figure south of the border."

"Regrets?"

"Oh, maybe, at first. I was young and stupid[352] and some share of some millions looked good. But a life on the run?"

"No thanks?"

"Yeah. No thanks. And life here? Now is good. Did I tell you I met a wonderful woman named Jill?"

"Happy for you, Stan. We all need somebody to love[353]."

****

NOTE: I've wanted to tell this story for decades but finally found a slot. I *was* a participant in the above conversation. I abstained and have no idea if they succeeded but I haven't seen them since. The idea *was* advanced by a man actually named Aubrey (RIP[354]).

---

352 See page 173, first sentence.
353 Reminding us of Grace Slick and the Jefferson Airplane®.
354 Or so I was told by his niece many years later.

Octopied

Most of us think obsidian tool[355]-making only goes back, oh, I dunno, maybe 500,000 years. Am I right? We're inclined to think that back before that it was all clubs and stone hammers.

That's entirely reasonable for we who grew up watching *The Flintstones* while being told that *Homo neandertalensis* was a species of stupid brutes. Sure, we carry traces of their DNA in our genome, but some stupid brutes successfully pitch a little woo even today. Maybe they were considered buff. Muscular, y'know?

Neanderthals wandered off from our line, headed for eventual extinction, somewhere between 300 and 800 thousand years ago. Opinions vary. In any event, they and we were clubbers and stoners back then, as some still are.

But just this morning[356] I read a report on vice.com® that blew me away! Paleoanthropologists working in Ethiopia have discovered a volcanic glass tool factory dating back 1.2 million years! They've uncovered almost 600 obsidian axes!

Moreover, this discovery *not only* takes obsidian tool making back more than 500,000 years, it suggests that our entire understanding of ancient cultures is turned on its head. In essentially all of the proto-human hominin sites previously examined, all of the functions of a clan were carried out in one place. They slept, they cooked, they ate, they sat around the fire playing their guitars, they sang, they doodled on cave walls, *and they fashioned their tools in the same little cave on the prairie!*

But there in Melka Kunter, Upper Awash, Ethiopia, the denizens, possibly *Homo erectus* or *Homo ergaster,* had a workshop separate from home sweet home! This suggests a level of social organization previously attributed to people like us—you know, *smart* people—not primitive creatures with brains about half the size of ours. *We're* the ones with sweat shops and unions!

---

355 Reminding us of the obsidian knives that were so present, perhaps to an excess, in the wild and wooly tales in *Cede Catalog-giving it all away,* BUB, 2021.

356 29 January, 2023. The Vice® story was published two days ago and linked to a paper published in December in *Nature Ecology & Evolution®*.

But why am I telling you all this? Isn't the current volume supposed to be a mish-mash of fiction? Bingo! Now we can move along to the good part which takes place about, oh, say 2 million years in the future.

You see, recent studies have found that octopodes are smarter than we thought and even use tools!

Also, if we get into runaway climate change this planet is going to become a water world after the poles melt and humans along with all other land animals go the way of the dodo.

Now we meet Plurp and Goba, a pair of paleooctopologists conducting studies in 5400000PIY (Post-Ice Year in the octal[357] number system). Given that most readers probably aren't fluent in Post-Inundation Octolect, I'll translate.

> Plurp: "These stone tools were being used by our ancestors almost 58300000 years ago."
>
> Goba: "Is that possible? That isn't long after our kind left their helmets behind."
>
> Plurp: "Even the nautili, the proto-octopids to which you refer, had a sort of intelligence. So, once freed from their heavy shell burden our line's brains must have expanded quickly."
>
> Goba: "This pushes our stone age lineage back 4500000s of years!"
>
> Plurp: "Indeed it does! I've submitted a sandscript doc to the *Journal of Octopid Origins* and it's being circulated tentacle to tentacle for peer review."
>
> Goba: "Congratulations dear friend! This will make you famous! You'll be one of the top 8 in our field! Give me 21!" [17 suction cups, in base 8] They slap arms.
>
> Plurp: "Thanks. Now how is your research coming along on those odd skeletal remains you discovered? Those bulbous globes with sockets and hinged mandibles? No evidence of gills. How could such creatures live in the sea? They clearly were not fish."
>
> Goba: "My theory is that they came here from another world and simply couldn't survive in this paradise."
>
> Plurp: "Good luck with that. I don't know anyoct who believes life is possible outside our glorious ocean."

---

[357] Base 8. Unlike the *Guna* people discussed on page 28, octopods can count their arms pretty accurately. In base 8, as in base 10, each place represents a factor. So 5 in the example represents 1×8^8, 4 represents 1×8^7 and so forth. You do the math.

Geocaching®²

Jill thought things over during the week and tossed a coin, leaving the crucial decision up to "everything that's unfolded since the Big Bang." Yesterday[358] she joined Stan for another go[359]. It was just a little chilly but wonderfully sunny and a fine day for a search party.

Her generous guide let Jill pick the next site and the GPS pointed to the Looking Glass Rock® trail a half hour or 45 minutes southeast of town in the Pisgah National Forest®.

Stan looked at his companion's feet. "Good," he observed.

"Good?"

"Footwear."

"Thanks. I mean, really, they're just shoes."

"But sturdy. Sturdy matters for a 5-1/2 mile round-trip hike that goes up 1600 feet in elevation."

"Sounds challenging. Should I pick another spot?"

"No. We're up to it. We're <u>young</u> and we're <u>strong.</u> But it means we'll be spending much of the day together. Are you up for *that?*"

"I'm good to go.[360]"

They stopped at the co-op to pick up sandwiches and water. [General Rule #16: "Food and water are a super good idea when undertaking a long walk in the woods."]

"I've been to Looking Glass before but not since I started 'caching[361]. Great view."

"Sounds lovely."

They talked of this and that as new friends usually do. I'd guess you have a pretty good idea of how that goes so I won't bore you with a transcription here.

She said. He said. He joked. She laughed, thinking he was fun and funny as Andrea had suggested. He was finding her to be

---

358 Saturday, 28 January, 2023

359 Page 169 if you've been jumping around in here. These stories really *are* in a well planned sequence. Just sayin'.

360 Evincing the serene side we explored on page 166. See what I mean about sequencing? Also she was cool with his implied underlining.

361 Those with experience tend to use this contraction.

copacetic.[362]

Stan parked at the trailhead, put the food in a day pack, locked up and said, "Onward and upward!"

The first part of the trail rises slowly after crossing a wooden bridge and then gets a good bit steeper climbing up to the summit. Both our protagonists were breathing a little harder as they hiked.

Stan checked his phone at intervals. "We don't know where the cache might be, but it's still ahead. We needn't start a search until we're pretty close."

"Seems like anything artificial would stick out like a sore thumb in this place. Like this," she said picking up a candy wrapper and stuffing it in her jeans pocket.

[Stan notes her solid environmental ethic.] "True, but the cache could be tucked in a nook."

"Or a cranny."

"That too."

The trail passed through and under a rhododendron thicket, between the reddish trunks and Jill said, "This must be gorgeous in bloom!"

"Maybe we should come back next summer." [He's hopeful.] "Or better still, visit the pink beds."

"I've heard they're pretty astounding."

"Indeed."

The GPS led them on. About 2 miles in they came to a flat expanse of bare rock.

"This is where EMS lands their helicopter if they need to rescue us."

"Are we in danger?"

"Not hiking. But some rock climbers have fallen. You'll see how they might when we reach the bald. The steep part is just ahead. Let's take a short break here."

Fifteen minutes later they continued the climb and soon reached the summit, then started down a short way, and, before long, broke out of the trees.

"Wow! What a view!" They were standing the top of the massive sloping cliff. "I get the falling thing. But what a view!"

Stan pointed across the valley. "That's the Blue Ridge Parkway®. Not open now. Winter conditions. But from there, particularly in the early morning, when the sunlight first hits here, you understand the name. Glows like a mirror. Mica I

---

362 Reminding us of the Vonnegut quote on page 159. Sequence counts.

guess."

"Let's do that sometime." [Making Stan even more hopeful.] "I mean, if you want to."

"Sounds good. Let's eat before we search."

So the pair sat on the smooth granite, lunched and chatted. He said. She said. She said. He laughed. Etc.

While they ate, a flock of vultures sailed into view soaring, nearly stationary in the updraft from the cliff face. One suddenly dived, swooped around and back up into the flock. Then another and another repeated the act.

"Like they're playing."

"Almost like they're dancing on the wind," Jill replied.

Then out came the phone again. "Hmm. Seems to be over that way." They walked slowly until he added. "Somewhere right around here."

There were numerous boulders and some dwarfed and gnarled trees with plenty of possible hidey holes. They split up, circling and peering, on their knees at times.

Suddenly Stan shouted, "I'm slipping! Afraid to move!"

Jill seeing that he had slid backwards on the rock, looked around, found a large broken branch and dragged it toward her partner. "Grab this!"

He couldn't quite reach it and she hazarded a step forward feeling throughly unserene. Now he got one hand on it and she pulled, almost starting to slide on her knees. Very gradually she was able to get her feet under her and drag him to where he found some traction until finally he was safe. He threw his arms around her and she could feel that he was trembling. "You saved my life."

"You owe me one."

"Gotta get some new boots. Tread's about gone on these."

"Good plan."

"Meanwhile, as I slid I saw something in that juniper over there."

They went to the tree and found a 35mm film container wedged in a crotch. "Open it!"

Inside they found a list with only two other names, plus a note.

BE EXTRA CAREFUL UP HERE!

"You can say that again!"

"Be extra careful, Stan. If you'd plunged to your death with the car keys in your pocket how would I have gotten home?"

The problem with earthworms[363]

"What?" [I hear you thinking.] "What?" [And, no, we aren't headed back into that crazy-making talk about gravity.] [Page 147.]

I didn't see any problem until just yesterday.[364] As a gardener I've always thought of *them* as part of the *solution*. I'm happy when I turn over soil and see a lot of them and a little sad when I inadvertently cut them in half.[365] Little did I know.

You see, prior to European entry there weren't *any* earthworms in North America. *Any*. Think about that. I'll wait.

...

So these days? They're pretty much *everywhere* if there's enough dirt on top of bedrock or gravel. Furthermore, they didn't get there on their own. Oh no. Advertently or inadvertently we spread them around. It's not like they have legs, y'know.

But, a problem? Don't they aerate the soil and increase absorption of rainwater? Don't they consume leaf mold and other vegetative waste at the surface and deposit worm poop downstairs?

Yes and yes and yes and yes.

"Is that a problem?" [Keep 'em coming!] [The questions, I mean.]

Yes and no.

Anyway, what I intended to title this little story, and had, in fact already typed upstairs early yesterday—before I stumbled on an entirely new way to view worms—was "The long and the short of it.[366]" [Maybe I'll use that later.]

What I intended to do was to catch you up on Greg Samsa

---

363 If I'd known this a month ago footnote #300 would have been altered.
364 1 February, 2023. Happy New Month!
365 See reference on page 42.
366 Though, come to think of that, it wouldn't be a bad name for a story about earthworms, say, cutting them in half for use as bait. Also, now that I've learned that worms are basically undocumented immigrants—no "green cards"—I may have to rethink my feelings about bait.

who we first met in the fanciful title story in the collection *Fifty Wheys to Love Your Liver*. (BUB®, 2018)

We recall that Greg kicked off the current cycle of stories (this being the 7th amalgamation since my muse "went seriously south" and launched me on the current precarious story-spinning flight-path) with his cockamamie idea that a book offering naturopathic cottage cheese recipes aimed at the health food crowd would make him rich and famous. Yeah. Right.

But the concept did lead to his *arrangement de deux*[367] with Kris leading to his partial ownership of a goat dairy and his full ~~ownership of~~ partnership with a talking Angus heifer named Macallan. And so forth, including, eventually, Macallan's twin.

[That's a story you oughtn't have missed.]

Ownership of the goat dairy leading to ... but no spoilers here. A lot can happen in 5 years, so we'll skip over those admittedly happy times.

Lately Greg has faced a bit of angst. Or bother. Rather, angsty bother. [Bothersome angstiness?]

:-(← (Graphic book judges, please note! Sad face.)

As we also recall, Greg's day job was that of a licensed electrician. (For any youngsters out there who've stayed up this late, do note that there are many career options that pay less and demand more. Why just this morning I was paid $40 for a 15 minute electrical repair!) [True fact.]

Well, former "day job." Once he started milking goats twice daily Greg's electrical work became more of a "midday job." Also, since he became the *de facto* talent agent for Mac, he only does electrical work a couple of middays per week in between making cheese, though Chelsea does her share when she's not teaching yoga classes in Asheville.[368] But enough about all that.

Before we get to the grim information hinted at four paragraphs north of here, I suppose I should note that Greg is *very* familiar with earthworms. Between the goats and the heifers and the foliage (weeds and waste) from an organic garden, Greg has a splendid compost pile, which, after heating up and cooling down, is thick with wiggly worms. (When he spreads the stuff on the garden he's always careful to do it on an overcast day so the little undocumented aliens don't cook before they can go subsurface. He's just that kind of guy.)

Oh, I see a hand up. What?

---

367 *Français!* About damn time!
368 See stories in *Seize You on the Dark Side of the Moo,* BUB®, 2019.

"Exactly. What's the problem?"

You mean for Greg?

"No, the title problem."

Oh, right. What I read about three days ago?

"No, you said 'yesterday.' Not three."

It *was* yesterday when I said that. Surely you don't think writing of this caliber emerges all at once, like some sort of Venus on a half-shell.[369] It takes time, like the green stuff growing on leftovers in the back of my fridge.

Actually, I've already answered your question in footnote #365, but I'll have another go in footnote #370.[370]

Where was I? Oh, Greg.

Right. If we think way back we recall that the original owner, well, not exactly original, but pretty far back, of Twinkleland®[371] (the goat dairy farm name), was Kris who had a

---

369 Reminding one of the science fiction novel *Venus on the Half Shell,* by "Kilgore Trout," the fictional writer in Kurt Vonnegut's *God Bless You Mr. Rosewater,* which novel contained a fragment of the fictional manuscript. With Vonnegut's permission the American writer Philip José Farmer expanded the fragment into a full length book. Dell Publishing®, 1975. (Now deemed a classic and quite pricey.)

370 Earthworms are Old World, delivered to the New World unintentionally [most likely] in flower pots or perhaps ballast offloaded from ships. While they seem all nice and normal today, they are anything but. The annelid invasion literally upended North American ecosystems. Whereas leaf mold previously piled up on forest floors, the barbarians snuck up from underneath when the leaves least expected it, ate their lunch—so to speak—and went back to their underground lairs to poop. This top-down conveyance radically changed conditions on the surface which was then less damp, more prone to run-off—though the tunnels somewhat offset this effect—and hotter. The microbial and insect life thereupon was altered as well which meant a shift in the food supply for birds and other insectivores. Meanwhile the nutrients formerly found upstairs were parked in the basement. The vegetative cover changed to species better able to survive in the new environment which necessarily changed the food supply for birds and mammals accustomed to the previous smorgasbord of nuts, fruits and berries.

On the plus side, if you like things they way they are now, they're nature's little helpers. As Vonnegut asked somewhere upslope, "If this isn't nice, what is?"

371 This was the name of my father's Shetland sheep dog kennel which he sold before I was born, yet was the source of my first companion: Suncall Scot of Twinkleland®—Scotty to me. Anyway, with Dad and

hot'n'steamy with Greg on page 23 of *Fifty Wheys*.

Then she had a change of heart, or at least gender preference, and ran off with Genna (page 25 of 50WTLYL). Her years with Greg had been great, and those with Genna good as well, but things didn't ultimately work out and now she's headed back to North Carolina.

Recall also that while Kris had cancelled the sex scene she was still half partner in the aforementioned Chapter S corporation that owned Twinkleland®.

Now, do know, she harbors no judgement regarding Greg's *histoire d'amour* with Chels nor any intentions in the way of restoring her-and-his previous hot'n'steamies—after all, she was the one who moved out—but she wants to move back in. Residentially.

NOTICE: Reading is dangerous. I just finished[372] with Charles Mann's *1493*, and down toward the end read about giant earthworms in the Philippines. Went to Wikipedia to confirm. This kills all my musing upslope. Filipino (and other Asian) worms go 27 inches. Take that Ms. Sherlock![373] Dave was nixed for naught.

Regarding Greg? I'm sure you can imagine.

Scotty long gone I used the name for the dairy because it's kinda nice.
372 Tuesday, 7 February, 2023, 9:37 p.m.
373 Page 146. Brit worm-lengths are so lame.

The long and the short of it

OK. OK. We've still got the title, but the rationale, as previously stated, was to catch you up on Greg. Now here we are, already caught up with our electrician-cum-goatherd, with the title still in play. [Jeez this authorship thing is difficult.]

So maybe I should catch you up with Macallan?

He's kind of a minor media star these days.

Macallan—the first publicly touted conversational cow—has made quite a splash, what with his radio talk show and so forth.

The thing, or at least "a" thing, was that no one other than Greg had previously accepted, or acceded to, conversation with a supposedly "dumb" beast. Who the hell knows how many other cows had spoken to their "owners?" Outspoken but unheard. [Rather "unherd?"] Because we know that farm-types are dyed in the wool "practical." Agriculture is science coupled with experience and "hearing voices" when one is tending livestock is pretty easily tossed aside as "just my imagination."

And those "lowings" in the Christmas carol about the manger? Were they talking about the unusual goings on in the barn?

Also, it would make most folks—well, many, at least—uncomfortable to send a conversational companion to the abattoir. [Not all. See the 7th graf on page 186.]

Then too, it may be that most other animals share in what I've previously described as feline *omerta,* given that cats know—but don't say. [Consequences are rumored to be severe.]

So Mac is the only heifer *I've heard of* with a radio talk show (have you?) and I wouldn't be surprised if most of his listeners believe he's a fake—say, a Scots actor with a delightful burr and a somewhat barnyard sense of humor. A fake albeit an *entertaining* fake.

What attentive listeners will have noticed, however, is that Mac is what you might call a classical liberal humanist. Well, bovinest I suppose. Liberal and conflicted (as aren't we all?)

Belief in democracy and self-determination and equal rights is easy to espouse but not as easy in actualization. Every cow for themself[374] bumps into herd mentality as soon as a charismatic leader emerges and the masses stampede toward the latest fad.

Then, too, there's the question of diet. As we noted in *Seize You on the Dark Side of the Moo,* Mac has boundaries regarding advertisers on his show. Chic-fil-A®? Yes. He appreciates their tongue-in-cud billboards.[375] McDonald's®? Nope. Beef is *not* what's for dinner.

Oh, he'll say—and has often said—that a vegan diet is best and that he's a *shining example.* But he's wise enough to understand that omnivory is natural for some. A heritable trait. Bing!

General Rule #17: "Omnivory is a heritable trait."

So, like any fair-minded classical liberal bovinist (F-MCLB) he's suggested that eating lower on the food chain is the responsible choice—fish and chicken, say, if alfalfa isn't your thing.

His sometime "veganer than thou" stance gets a little squishy when you ask him about insects. "How do you avoid eating pancrustacean hexapod invertebrates while you graze?"

Silence.

"Cat got your tongue?" [Note the interspecial angle here.]

"Ye gat me there, sonny. Not like oi've meself an opposable thumb fer the pickin' of bugs from *mo suipeir*[376]."

"Making you an *uilebheist?*[377]"

"*Chan eil,*[378] sonny. Not by choice."

Fair enough. And I wouldn't want you to think less of him. He's a good person.[379]

We recall that he learned to speak thanks to the somewhat rebellious farm wife who read Shakespeare® to him and his brother when they were wee wads. She knew it was *wrong* to teach chattel to talk, but they were *so cute!* And they nuzzled her after she'd given them a handful of sweet feed! Her husband would have been *sgith*[380] if he'd known, but Mac and his bro were

---

374 That pesky plural "them" again. Sheesh! "Itself?"
375 As an "it" Mac is not much tuned in to the anti-gay posture of Chic's management. He's not faultless.
376 First use of Scots Gaelic in the current volume! "My supper."
377 Again. "Omnivore" in the highlands.
378 Again. "No." Are we on a roll, or what?
379 In the sense that any thinking being,—or mattress for that matter— qualifies for personhood. F-MCLB and so forth.
380 Once more. "Peeved." The couple were Scots emigres.

mum when the farmer was at hand.

It was thanks to her that Mac was a feminist before he became bovinist and he didn't understand for quite a bit that he was also a heifer. [The kindly couple numbed their chattel prior to castration.] But once having understood, Mac became an 'it-ist." "I am an it!" he proclaimed, "Not a she-he earthworm!"

Once inflamed with a passion for literature Mac had gone deep. He learned that Willie Shakespeare had been profoundly influenced by Montaigne, particularly the latter's foundational essay "On Cruelty."

"Sonny," Mac said to me, "It's wha that bright-light Adam Gopnik® writ in *A Thousand Small Sanities*."

"That wasn't published until 2019," I retorted.

"Did ye think I've stopt reading?" Mac snorted. "Is nae as if I'm a pancrustacean hexapod invertebrate trapt in amber."

"Touché. So what did this Gopnik[381] guy have to say?"

"We can always rationalize our way past someone else's suffering.[382]"

Isn't that the truth? And yet there is General Rule #17. [A naturopathic P.A. told me many years ago that the sickest people she encountered in her practice were the vegans. So there's that.] Humans are innately omnivorous and vegans maintain good health only by way of vitamin B-12 supplements or the consumption of <u>unwashed</u> root vegetables.

The grit! Oh, the gritty grit!

And who knows what microbial life forms inhabit an unwashed carrot? (Well, obviously an agronomist, but you? Me?) Which arguably makes veganism a concept in the mind of the beholder. (Carrot-holder?) Micro-omnivory writ small.

<u>Note:</u> I am self-aware enough to see that I may well be rationalizing my way past suffering, but I was a vegan for 8 years some decades ago and know whereof I speak.

The grit! Oh, the grit!

[The lack of an opposable thumb—and fingers for that matter—is why Mac has to dictate his weekly blog posts, and while voice transcription has come a long way, between spell-check and his brogue, corrections are a constant issue. See below.]

---

381 *A Thousand Small Sanities,* Basic Books®, 2019, p. 30.

382 See reference to *post hoc* reasoning on page 127. This is one of the enduring themes in the present volume and will recur in the Book Club Questions somewhere down slope.

But we want deeper, do we not? Eat alfalfa? Eat a cow?

Mac has transcended. [He's past his cud, so to speak. Also "passed." Cow pies, burps, farts etc. Which Ronald Reagan not entirely wrongly blamed for climate change.]

[Also, as noted in *Fifty Wheys to Love Your Liver*,[383] Reagan called ketchup in school lunches a "vegetable."]

[A vegetable!]

[Corrective note: A tomato is a fruit. So ketchup is arguably a form of heat-reduced, flavored fruit juice.]

So. Greg is pretty darn busy between the goats, the cheese, the soap, the garden, the intermittent electrical work and managing Mac's production schedule and syndication. [Makes me a little weary just imagining that juggle.]

And while Chelsea pitches in, she has her life to lead. Being a yoga instructor probably sounds all dreamy and downward dog and cobra posey, but it involves a lot of counseling. Students bring their troubles along with their mats and water bottles and expect their centered and flexible tutor to *listen*. [That, too, wearies me, just thinking about it.]

Still, Chelsea tackled Mac's edits for some years and she's grown quite fond of the beast.

But now Kris is back. We didn't think of this until just this very minute,[384] but Kris was an *English major* before she fell in love with what's-his-name who had inherited the farm! [Guess I should go back and find that. Give me a minute.]

...

[Oh, right. Herman, who subsquently ran off with the woman who peddled handmade brooms at the tailgate market, then, later ran off with another woman. That's the rut wherein Herman's stuck.]

We here note that none of us is getting younger. Gosh! Greg is 62 now, and Chels is 57. Kris is in her mid-sixties and her once red pony tail is greying. She still has those charming freckles, and flashing green peepers. Her formerly lithesome figure is only a little worse for wear.[385]

Greg's angst was misplaced it seems. Kris and Chels have hit it off famously and do their matted poses together every morning! Kris, of course, knows the goat biz from horn-tip to tail

---

383 Did I mention this was published in 2018?
384 5:04:37 a.m., 19 January, 2023
385 I recovered these physical details when I went back to *50 Wheys* to find Herman's name. I'd forgotten many of these things in the past 5 years.

and jumped right in.

While Kris and Greg had exchanged e-mails from time to time, including, of course, the surprising discovery of Mac's linguistic acumen, talking with him took things to a new level. I mean, she'd listened to the podcasts, but those are not as tangible as hearing him up close and personal.

So Kris offered to take on the copy editing of the blog which further endeared her to Chels.

Here's a sample. First the original:

"Tisn't as if ye begettin' uile[386] that ye be wanton on the first outin ye no? Nae.[387] Life is as gude as ye make oft and as yer song woman Joni placed it, greed is the unraveling."

Then Kris's revision:

"It isn't as if you'll get all that you hope for on the first attempt, you know? Nae.[388] Life is only as good as you make it and as your song writer Joni framed it, "Greed is the unraveling. It's the unraveling and it undoes all the joy that could be. I want to have fun, I want to shine like the sun I want to be the one that you want to see."[389]

No person—no cow[390] for that matter—can fail to benefit from the attention of a good editor. Bing!

General Rule #18: We all need good editors.

---

386 Scots Gaelic again.
387 Ditto.
388 Ditto. We see here that Kris is a sensitive enough editor that she retains the original *"Nae"* to lend linguistic flavor.
389 And here Kris embraces editorial license to offer up what she knew Mac *intended to convey* in his abbreviated quote. "All I Want," Joni Mitchell, *Blue,* A&M®, 1971. If this seems like extreme editorial meddling you should have read Thom Wolfe's *Look Homeward, Angel: A Story of the Buried Life,* before *his* editor got hold of it!
390 Rereading footnote #379 I see that the distinction offered in this sentence is redundant. We've already established that Mac is a person due to his observed intellect.

'Til the end of time

[If I don't get cranking I'm not going to come up with 20 General Rules before the trap door on this stage opens, and I may not hit my "all time record goal" of 400 footnotes in a single volume.]

Jeannette Éttiene may be able to help. Her great great great something was Éttiene Louis Geoffroy®, a French entomologist and pharmacist in the 18th century—though how his first name became her last is a mystery lost in the gloaming shadows of time.[391] Basically, his name was "Steve" *en français*, so ~~Jeannie~~ Jeannette is kind of a Jean Stevens. Or Stephens.

Geoffroy was keen on beetles, and why not? As J.B.S. Haldane® supposedly told a gathering of theologians who asked him what the study of nature suggested about the Creator he was reportedly said to have replied: "He has an inordinate fondness for beetles."[392]

There are at least 400,000 species known and it's anybody's guess how many more are out there, so Geoffroy had a pretty wide-open field. Given the odd state of pharmacology at that time he may have had *a lot* of leisure hours to pursue bugs. He subscribed to astrological herbology, which somehow connected the effective relationship of plant-based derivatives to sun signs.

Uh-huh.

Astrology has eternally proved to be right <u>every once in a while.</u> Or, at least, nearly so. [Newspaper astrology is generally vague enough that one size fits all. Kind of like coin flipping to place horse race bets.] So repeat business might have been thin, though one must suppose credulity was as common then as now. Curing people from time to time is not, generally, a strong sales driver. "Ah, that fella Steve? He saved my cousin from a sorry case of the heebeejeebies."]

Bingo!

---

391 Likely something to do with marriage or other trauma. I recall that the namesake branch of my family, evicted from Scotland in the 1700s, didn't have a "family" name until they landed in Ireland and identified themselves with the area where they'd been evicted. Bothwell, Scotland.
392 Though, like many "famous quotes," this has been attributed to others.

General Rule #19: "Astrology is right, occasionally."

It will likely come as a complete surprise that ~~Jeannie~~ Jeannette is a friend of our boy in the fire tower, Terry.[393] She's one of very few people he's told about his mattress theory, though, obviously, once the present book is short-listed for the National Book Award® the idea will gain great currency.

~~Jeannie~~ Jeannette doesn't exactly *subscribe* to the mattress theory, but she's open minded. She has read Gould®[394] and accepts his research into Haldane's statement, which Gould® found in a secretarially recorded presentation by J.B.S.® on the possibility and potential source of extraterrestrial life.

"Inordinate fondness" is a lovely turn of phrase but must be credited to some subsequent editor.[395] Haldane®, per the recorded minutes, suggested that life might be attributed to the supernatural, might have emerged from inorganic materials, or could be a constituent part of the universe.

If it were the first, he noted, given that there are 400,000 species of beetles and only 8,000 mammals, "the Creator, *if he exists,* has a special preference for beetles." [My italics, not, perhaps, his.] [One can dream]

This, of course, raises the possibility—one which seems most likely to ~~Jeannie~~ Jeannette—that when we are finally visited by beings from a galaxy far, far away, they will likely have six legs and sturdy carapaces. Nor does she attribute this so much to the possibly supernatural as to the fact that bugs with armor are survivors.

"Just look," she says. "Just look at how U.S. soldiers in Iraq and Afghanistan were buying their own body armor. Or their families holding bake sales to buy it for them. Those soldiers didn't come home in a box.[396] Mostly." [Reminds me somehow of Beetle Baily® who apparently survived WWII. At least in ink.]

Hard to argue with that.

She'd be the first to admit that Terry's idea is, in some ways, more appealing, since sleeping on a squirming pile of beetles doesn't exactly sound comfy. But she has good reasons. How reasonably comfy, limbless mattresses would be able to build mechanical transport is a puzzle within a riddle, whereas beings

---

393 Page 13, etc.
394 Also a Stephen. Stephen Jay as it happens.
395 A fine example of what a good editor can do for one's reputation.
396 This a reference to Country Joe & the Fish®, "I Feel Like I'm Fixin' to Die Rag," Woodstock, '69.

with six limbs and a shell have two legs up on people like us and are inherently inured to many of the slings and arrows of outrageous fortune.

[Beetles got us coming and going. Though we are often told that cockroaches will be the principle survivors of a future nuclear war, it is pretty clear that beetles have the inside track.[397]]

Then, too, ~~Jeannie~~ Jeannette is deep. Not deep in the shallow way exhibited by Randy back on page 134, but really deep.

She's a student of set theory!

I can practically hear the whoosh of your helpless gasp.

"Really?" you ask.

Do you think I make this stuff up?

[Oh, by the way, I just figured out how Geoffroy's first name became ~~Jeannie's~~ Jeannette's last.]

Okay, the thing with sets is that a set can consist of anything. It started in mathematics with statements like {x:where x is the group of all numbers evenly divisible by 17}. You know, the kind of stuff we all run into when we're shopping for groceries or sitting on a river bank with a line in the water.

But it grew, as things will. A set can include {my cats, your dog} or {all humans who have read all of my books}. [Three and 1 respectively.]

Fair enough. ~~Jeannie~~ Jeannette goes the extra mile, though, and mulls Russell's Paradox®. Sets can contain a contradiction! Bertrand Russell® tripped over this more than a hundred years ago, and unlike, say, astrological herbology, it still fascinates.

In layperson's terms it can be simply put: {this statement is false}. (We could work this out in numbers, but it would quickly get complicated, and complication is something we don't need. Trust me on this.)

When you think about it, as ~~Jeannie~~ Jeannette does, it seems kind of strange that it took so long. Mathematics seems to have climbed out of its cocoon around 3000 BCE in Macedonia, but it took 5,000 years before Russell had that light bulb pop up over his head.[398]

The thing is that unlike Fermi's Paradox®, Russell's will never resolve. At some point we will either be visited by

---

[397] Maybe this should have been a footnote?

[398] My guess is that the idea was lurking during all those centuries but was out of sight before Thomas Alva Edison® invented the light bulb in 1879. Then it only took about 20 years.

mattresses or beetles from a galaxy far, far away, or—assuming we don't first get wiped out by an asteroid, climate change or a really nasty pandemic—humans or our descendant species will visit all the planets in the multiverse and find or not find other life forms. [This may take awhile. In any case, the answer is discoverable.]

But: {this statement is false}? No way.

I see a hand up. Yes?

"Her family name?"

Well, at least one of you has been paying attention.

See, ~~Jeannie~~ Jeannette was married, and as is often the case took her husband's last name. Townsend. When they divorced she decided to change her name, legally I mean. She had grown up as Jean Stevens, but she thought that sounded pretty Plain Jane, or Plain Jean if you will. Since she was going to go through the rigamarole involved in the switch and because she had read about her great, great, great whatever, and because she thinks beetles are cool, and so forth, she asked the judge to rename her Jeannette Éttiene. This, you see, pays homage to both her original family name and her ancestor, plus it sounds more elegant.

Thus it isn't exactly a "family" name. Just hers. Unique!

Actually, she just now asked me to not use hypocoristics, and to go back and use her "real" name. Will do, Jeannette, will do. [Have just gone back and struck through and replaced the offenders.]

OK. Nothing above this sentence, back to page 189, is the "story" part of this story, other than giving you some background on our heroine—for heroine she is!

Jeannette saved a life!

She was minding her own business last week, headed home after a long day at the office.

Her day job is with the U.S. Forest Service®—which is how she met Terry by the way—though she now works at a different office than Carol Saarinen. [I'm sure you remember Carol, executor of boustrophedon?]

Come to think of it, she used to have Carol's current job but was promoted. Whereas Carol currently deals with the limited set {all of the trees in her section} Jeannette now treats with {all of the trees in this forest}.[399]

I see another hand up and I know what you're wondering.

Were Terry and Jeannette itemized at some point? Am I right? I see you nodding.

---

399 A large number. And whooeee! We're almost there!

Not really. They went out a few times and became fast friends but didn't click romantically, or to put a finer point on it, sexually. Not every checkout leads to a hook-up. [Tempted to make this a General Rule, but want to save #20 for something more important. Also tempted to make this a footnote rather than a parenthetical comment, but saving #400 for the same reason.]

Where was I? Oh, right, headed home.

Those of you who drive have doubtless experienced being on automatic, your thoughts far, far away as you follow the regular route home. It's not that you aren't paying attention to your driving, but you aren't thinking "this is where I turn," or "the light is red," or "this is a 4-way stop."

Well, that was Jeannette last Wednesday (1 March, 2023). [I know I have put most—maybe all—reference dates in footnotes up to now, but as I said upslope, am saving the next one. Best for last is my rule.]

She was mulling Russell's Paradox® as she piloted her Leaf® toward home. [I thought it appropriate for a Forest Service® employee to drive a Leaf®.]

"If it's true it isn't. If it's not true it is."

You can see why this would tangle someone up.

So, she was headed up Merrimon and side-stepped into the left-turn lane at WT Weaver—a new traffic pattern only lately put in place. Thence WT Weaver to Barnard for a righty. Therefrom a 20 mph crawl up Barnard to Edgewood, and across Edgewood to the wye that connects to Lookout Rd. Thence to my front door.

Yes. I confess. All of my important characters live with me. The mental house is pretty crowded. Double bunked to the max.

[That's why Jeannette and so many others have followed that same trajectory after work or a hike or celebration. We've all got that route down pat.]

Jeannette next bumped into Stan and Patsy who, as usual, were kind of all about paint. I guess this is the first time I've noted that S&P became a "thing." Then not, though it went great guns for a spell.

"Yikes" how does an author keep track?

But after the hot'n'steamy trailed off they have remained good friends—one on the tall ladder the other low—which is how Jeannette happened to bump into them both at the same time. They had just finished painting the east side of my house. Which needed it. [Method in my madness you see. I let them live here if they make themselves useful.]

Jeannette pointed at Stan. "Hey chum. There's paint on

your forehead." [Possibly making him part of the set: {People with paint on their foreheads}.]

He quipped, "Is that a subset of: {this statement is true} or {this statement is untrue}?

Then Patsy told a calculus joke and they all had a good laugh. [See pages 142-143. This too could have been a footnote, but I'm holding out! Also please note that all of my top of the line characters *love* calculus jokes.]

Stan said, "Hey ~~Jeannie~~ Jeannette! We're going to clean up and go to dinner at HomeGrown®, over on Merrimon. Join us?"

Jeannette turned to me and pointed at the sentence above, shaking her head. I nodded and fixed it.

"Sounds good," she answered.

So a half hour or so later the three headed off in Patsy's pickup. [Stan's is in the shop and Jeannette had to plug in her Leaf® since the battery was low.]

The thing about HomeGrown® is that they serve farm-to-table food in old fashioned ways with only the slightest modern upgrade. Trust me, the chicken and trout platters are great! And to whatever extent possible, depending on the season, the food is local. Jeannette had the former, Stan the latter, and Patsy picked a vegetarian option. Good choices all around!

Our forester told the others about the ten year plan that was approved at the end of December. "A hot mess," is her view. "Here we asked for public input, got thousands of responses almost all of which asked for more old growth protection, and the bosses put together a management deal that wipes out thousands of acres of oldies."

"Doesn't seem right," one of her companions said.

"Damn!" snapped the other.

"And it's my job to implement it."

"Can't you stop it?"

"I might be able to curb the worst ..." Jeannette trailed off. "But not much."

"Damn!" Patsy put a hand on her friend's arm. [This disambiguates the speakers in the 4th and 5th sentences upslope.] "That doesn't seem right." [Reambiguating. Oh well.]

"Who makes those decisions anyway?" Stan asked.

"Someone way up the ladder."

"Bet it's someone aiming for a corporate job when they bail out of government service. With some major forest products company." Patsy shook her head. "Are they all corrupt?"

"Maybe. But not the folks in my office. We do our best with

the jobs we're assigned. Curb the worst, I guess. But enough about work. What's up for the weekend?"

The conversation veered from there. The painters were set on two different concerts and Jeannette said her big event (she laughed) was laundry and possibly lunch with Terry.

"Terry?"

"Yeah, the fellow we met on page 13. Old friend. Works a fire tower 5 days a week, remember?"

"Lover?"

"No. A friend. Common interests."

"Trees?"

"Nah. That's work. We talk about life on other planets."

"Planning to move?"

"Hah. Just speculation. We both read a lot. Talk about how life began. You know, the usual stuff that a subset of Bothwell's people discuss: {People who think about how life began}.

"Doesn't it begin when a seed or an egg gets fertilized?"

"I guess for some folks that works. My sense is that life as we know it on earth only started once and the whole place has been jumping ever since. We have DNA that goes all the way back to the first single-celled whatchamacallit."

"Continuous chain."

"Right."

"Which would mean all the chatter about when it begins is horse pucky."

"Makes complete sense to me," Patsy rejoined.

The convo continued in this fascinating way through the meal and the drive home during which a heavy rainstorm blew in. The three of them were completely soaked just dashing from the truck to the front door where the cats and I greeted them.

"Raining cats out there," I observed.

"And dogs," Stan added.

"Only cats here y'know."

"Oh right."

The three of them took turns with hot showers and afterward Jeannette and Stan went into the living room and sat together on the sofa. [I think there might be some chemistry happening there which might easily lead to one final hot'n'steamy before we exit this tangled web.]

Patsy joined me in the kitchen. She nodded toward the other room. "Think they've clicked."

"Looks like it."

"He's a good man."

"Not jealous?"

"Nah. We had a little wild time but we have our differences. Finally the differences did it."

"Which were?"

"One really. One that mattered. I'm a uni- and he's a multi-. As in verse."

"Poetry?"

"No. Didn't you read 'Irked?' Back on page 75? I mean, you wrote it, right?"

"Oh, yeah. But that was 6 or 7 months ago. Things fade."

"Well Stan and I had a pretty big blow up after we read it. Our biggest. That's when he started sleeping on the futon."

"Oh, I wondered about that. Should we warn Jeannette?"

"She's a big girl. And what with her stuff about beetles from a galaxy far, far away, I'd guess she can handle some multi-. I just couldn't."

So the incipient love-birds stayed up pretty late though they didn't conjoin at bed time and the rain continued.

In the morning Stan was off early to a job over in West Asheville, a one story home so he didn't need his aerialist back-up. Patsy headed down to Biltmore to paint a kitchen.

Jeannette and I drank coffee and ate crepes before she went to her place of employ. She, as we've come to understand, is a francophile and crepes are her idea of a good time.

She had time to tell me about her distress over the new management plan which was how I was able to go back and insert it in the dinner convo on page 194. A top-notch writer needs informed sources to add verisimilitude to his fiction. Or hers.

I'm clearly sympathetic, having been one of the thousands of public commenters, and told her so.

"Thanks," she said. "We tried."

But then she had to go. She unplugged her Leaf®, headed down Lookout, left on Barnard, across Edgewood, 20 mph down hill to WT Weaver, left, then right on Merrimon and so forth. Again pretty much on automatic as she mulled.

"If it's true it isn't. If it's not true it is."

Soon enough she was at her office parking lot, and headed in for the daily grind. Plans, applications, permits, phone calls, texts, e-mails—the works.

Hand up? Yes?

"She saved a life?"

I was going to get to that, but we've hit 200 pages and there really isn't room. Oh, wait, there's that blank space on page 34.

Book Club Study Questions

1. Can you pronounce *post hoc?*
2. Are you sure?
3. If this isn't nice, what is?
4. When was the last time you tried to explain calculus to an ant?
5. Where do you think ideas come from?
6. Can you calculate your weight in bars of chocolate?
7. How much wood would a woodchuck chuck?
8. Are you telling the truth now?
9. Mattress: comfy accoutrement or alien life form?
10. Knock knock ...

Author Interview

Are you happy now?

"With what?"

With "What."

"What?"

The "what" in the story that starts on page 166.

"Oh, that what. Rather those whats."

Yes.

"I'd say I'm happy with some whats."

Really happy?

"Somewhat."

Is there anything you'd like to say in your own defense?

"I meant well."

Shameless Commerce Page

Lucky Breaks (breaking good)

If you loved this book, you need to read the prequel.[402] The stories here left you with a lot of questions. Unanswered questions. But now you know where to go. So go already.

402. And the pre-prequels, *Cede Catalogue: giving it all away*; *Self-Evident: We Hold These Tooths*; *Waist Not, Want Knot*; *Seize You on the Dark Side of the Moo*; and *Fifty Wheys to Love Your Liver.*

Whale Falls: An exploration of belief and its consequences

What do you believe and why? How do your beliefs affect your view of, and relationship with, the world? A very personal examination of the author's journey through a lifetime of adventure and abuse and resolution.

Find these and more at BraveUlysses.com. Or ask for them at your local indie bookseller!

CPSIA information can be obtained
at www.ICGtesting.com
Printed in the USA
LVHW020654250423
745210LV00009B/492